**No Longer the Property of
Tidewater Community College**

Archaeologies of Conflict

DEBATES IN ARCHAEOLOGY

Series editor: Richard Hodges

Against Cultural Property, John Carman
The Anthropology of Hunter Gatherers, Vicki Cummings
Archaeologies of Conflict, John Carman
Archaeology: The Conceptual Challenge, Timothy Insoll
Archaeology and International Development in Africa, Colin Breen and Daniel Rhodes
Archaeology and Text, John Moreland
Archaeology and the Pan-European Romanesque, Tadhg O'Keeffe
Beyond Celts, Germans and Scythians, Peter S. Wells
Combat Archaeology, John Schofield
Debating the Archaeological Heritage, Robin Skeates
Early European Castles, Oliver H. Creighton
Early Islamic Syria, Alan Walmsley
Gerasa and the Decapolis, David Kennedy
Image and Response in Early Europe, Peter S. Wells
Indo-Roman Trade, Roberta Tomber
Loot, Legitimacy and Ownership, Colin Renfrew
Lost Civilization, James L. Boone
The Origins of the Civilization of Angkor, Charles F. W. Higham
The Origins of the English, Catherine Hills
Rethinking Wetland Archaeology, Robert Van de Noort and Aidan O'Sullivan
The Roman Countryside, Stephen Dyson
Shipwreck Archaeology of the Holy Land, Sean Kingsley
Social Evolution, Mark Pluciennik
State Formation in Early China, Li Liu and Xingcan Chen
Towns and Trade in the Age of Charlemagne, Richard Hodges
Vessels of Influence: China and the Birth of Porcelain in Medieval and Early Modern Japan, Nicole Coolidge Rousmaniere
Villa to Village, Riccardo Francovich and Richard Hodges

Archaeologies of Conflict

John Carman

BLOOMSBURY
LONDON · NEW DELHI · NEW YORK · SYDNEY

Bloomsbury Academic

An imprint of Bloomsbury Publishing Plc

50 Bedford Square   175 Fifth Avenue
London   New York
WC1B 3DP   NY 10010
UK   USA

www.bloomsbury.com

First published 2013

© John Carman, 2013

All rights reserved. No part of this publication may be reproduced or transmitted in any form or by any means, electronic or mechanical, including photocopying, recording, or any information storage or retrieval system, without prior permission in writing from the publishers.

John Carman has asserted his right under the Copyright, Designs and Patents Act, 1988, to be identified as Author of this work.

No responsibility for loss caused to any individual or organization acting on or refraining from action as a result of the material in this publication can be accepted by Bloomsbury Academic or the author.

British Library Cataloguing-in-Publication Data
A catalogue record for this book is available from the British Library.

ISBN: HB: 978-1-84966-888-0

Library of Congress Cataloging-in-Publication Data
Carman, John, 1952-
Archaeologies of conflict / John Carman.
   pages cm
Includes bibliographical references and index.
ISBN 978-1-84966-888-0 (hardback)
1. Military archaeology. 2. Military art and science–History.
3. War–History. I. Title.
CC77.M55C37 2013
355–dc23
2012046561

Typeset by Newgen Imaging Systems Pvt Ltd, Chennai, India
Printed and bound in Great Britain

Contents

Preface	vi
Acknowledgements	ix
List of figures	x
List of tables	xi
Introduction	1
1　Archaeology and conflict studies	5
2　Prehistoric conflict	23
3　Battlefield archaeology	41
4　Modern conflict	63
5　The potential of Conflict Archaeology	81
Conclusion: Countering a critique of Conflict Archaeology	99
Bibliography	103
Index	131

Preface

A friend and colleague – knowing my interest in archaeologies of conflict – once asked: 'Do you like war then?' My answer was 'no' – and a fuller answer is available from a paper given at the CHAT (Contemporary and Historical Archaeology in Theory) conference in 2003 (Carman and Carman 2007).

I first entered the field of Conflict Archaeology – not completely wittingly, and before the field received a name – in 1991, when I undertook to edit a volume on the archaeological study of warfare and violence for Cruithne Press. I had initially volunteered to contribute to such a volume as a result of my longstanding interest in matters military, but the original editor passed on to a different project and I was invited to take over. The book finally saw the light of day as *Material Harm: Archaeological Studies of War and Violence* (Carman 1997). After completing my PhD (in an entirely separate field) in 1993, I sought a new project and the entry of battlefields into the category of 'heritage' in the 1990s caught my interest. Out of that grew the *Bloody Meadows Project* shared with Patricia Carman from 1995 (Carman and Carman 2006). A conference in 1996 – in Durham on prehistoric conflict – led to a collaboration with Anthony Harding and the co-edited volume *Ancient Warfare: Archaeological Perspectives* (Carman and Harding 2006) that can perhaps claim to represent the standard work on prehistoric warfare in Europe so far: it has since been reprinted twice.

Like many in the burgeoning field of battlefield research at that time, Patricia Carman and I were largely unaware of the growing interest that was developing. Like others, we offered what we thought would be an eagerly snapped-up paper to help fill a day at a conference on the topic to be held in Glasgow in 1999 and organized by Tony Pollard and Phil Freeman. The wealth of papers that were in fact offered – from all over the globe – caused a delay to that conference, which was held in the following year as the first of the *Fields of Conflict* conferences (Freeman and Pollard 2001). In the meantime, I had contributed to a session at the Fourth World Archaeological Congress in Capetown, South Africa, organized by John Schofield and others on the archaeology of modern conflict, which resulted in a further publication (Schofield et al. 2002). These various publications have given me a footing in all three main areas of conflict research in archaeology: prehistoric, historic and modern. It is these period divisions that provide the central structure for this book.

Quite by chance, in 2004, I gave a paper at a conference in Cambridge that mentioned the battlefield at Oudenaarde, one of those the *Bloody Meadows Project* had studied (Carman and Carman 2006, 78–81). As a result, we were invited by the Ename Center for Public Archaeology and Heritage Interpretation to become part of an advisory group for the commemoration of the battle to be held in 2008 (Lachaert 2008). The commemoration comprised three elements: a major exhibition about the city of Oudenaarde and the battle; a re-enactment weekend on the anniversary of the battle; and the *Fifth Fields of Conflict* conference, held in Ghent and Oudenaarde in October 2008, co-organized by Patricia Carman and myself with the Ename Center.

Out of the Oudenaarde collaboration have since emerged other projects that will be referred to in this book:

- an ongoing process of collaborative research into the Oudenaarde battlefield, one of the largest in Europe;
- the establishment of a register or inventory of battlefields in Flanders, akin to those in – or planned for – England, Scotland, Wales and Ireland;
- the foundation of the ESTOC (European Studies of Terrains of Conflict) group, comprising leading figures in battlefield archaeology from all across Europe; in turn developing

- a European register of historic battlefields; and
- guidelines on research into, conservation of and providing access to historic battlefields.

This book derives from this long involvement in Conflict Archaeology and the associations I have developed in the study of prehistoric conflict, historic battlefield research and modern conflict study. By having a place in all these three areas, I am one of the few able to give a complete overview of the development of Conflict Archaeology as a distinct branch of the discipline. The connections – or lack thereof – between the three periods provides a context for the MA in Conflict Archaeology established at the University of Birmingham in 2007. It also informs the work of a number of current PhD students, also based in the University of Birmingham, with whom I am privileged to work. The book aims not only to provide an overview of the current state of Conflict Archaeology internationally, but also to look beyond this to what Conflict Archaeology *could* be and the wider contribution it can make to the study of the past and beyond. Its ultimate purpose – in line with the purpose of the *Debates in Archaeology* series – is to promote debate and discussion within Conflict Archaeology circles and outside. I look forward to taking part in discussions of the issues it raises.

John Carman
Birmingham, March 2012

Acknowledgements

I am grateful to all those who have contributed to the origins and production of this book. Thanks are due to Dr Ross Samson, formerly of Cruithne Press, for inviting me to begin this journey; to Tony Pollard and Phil Freeman for founding the *Fields of Conflict* series of conferences, and to Doug Scott, Charlie Haecker, Larry Babits, Glenn Foard, Achim Rost and Susanne Wilbers-Rost and their own colleagues for continuing the series; to friends and colleagues in ESTOC; and to my students for encouraging me to think more deeply about this area of interest. The greatest thanks goes – as always – to Patricia Carman for her unwavering love and commitment, and for the partnership in life and work that has ensued.

List of figures

2.1 Evidence of conflict in multiple periods? Dunnideer Hillfort, Aberdeenshire: crowned by a medieval tower — 28

3.1 Survey on the battlefield of Oudenaarde, September 2011 — 42

4.1 Auschwitz II – Birkenau: a site of internment and extermination — 75

5.1 Fortress, trading post and residence: the 'French Castle' (seventeenth century), Old Fort Niagara, New York, USA — 83

5.2 Fortified church at Scy-Chazelles, Metz, France. 'Home' church of Robert Schumann, Mayor of Metz and co-founder of the European Union — 85

List of tables

2.1	Evidence for prehistoric warfare in Europe (after Keeley 1996)	26
2.2	Archaeological correlates for prehistoric warfare	29
2.3	Determinants of style of warfare versus causes of warfare in anthropological and archaeological literature	35
3.1	Methodologies of historic battlefield research	52

Introduction

The last two decades has seen the emergence of a specific set of archaeological approaches to warfare and conflict across the Anglophone world and beyond, so that it is emerging as a specific area of interest for archaeologists. For some it can be classed as an archaeological specialism in its own right, something that can be called Conflict Archaeology, although what precisely to call it has been the subject of debate, some of which continues. At the time of writing, the field boasts not only several regular conference series, as well as individual sessions at most major conferences, but also a dedicated journal, a growing number of accessible and widely available publications, and specialist postgraduate courses in universities. What the field of Conflict Archaeology so far lacks, however, is a single text outlining the achievements and limitations of the field as it has emerged. This is the gap this short book seeks to fill.

Although the study of prehistory was arguably never quite the 'pacified past' that some (e.g. Keeley 1996) have claimed, there was a clear rise of interest in prehistoric conflict from the 1990s, coincident with and possibly the result of the return of warfare to Europe after an absence of 50 years. The development of key methodologies for the study of battlefields – previously understood to be largely devoid of material evidence – in the United States in the 1980s inspired a generation of British and European archaeologists to turn their attention to sites in their own countries. The end of the Cold War and key anniversaries of the World Wars inspired others, especially in the United Kingdom, to examine the material legacy of those conflicts before they disappeared. By 2000, the study of war was firmly on the archaeological agenda and the number and range of studies has grown apace over the past decade.

This book reviews the development of the field of Conflict Archaeology with the intention of providing not only a historical assessment of the current state of the field, but also looking forward to what Conflict Archaeology could offer as it develops. The central argument – derived from the author's experience of involvement in Conflict Archaeology for two decades – is that at present Conflict Archaeology is effectively divided into closed communities that do not interact to any large extent. These separate communities are divided by period, so that prehistory, historic battlefields and modern conflict represent entirely different domains of enquiry. They are also separated by nationality, especially in the case of historic battlefield and modern conflict research, so that a truly international Conflict Archaeology has yet to emerge. These divisions prevent the exchange of information and ideas across the division boundaries and thereby limit the scope of the field to develop as it should. This book discusses these issues in detail. It clearly outlines how they affect the development of Conflict Archaeology as a coherent branch of archaeology.

The book also promotes the unification and globalization of the field by demonstrating the aspects of the different period divisions, which carry implications for the others and how they can usefully inform each other. Looking beyond archaeology to other fields that study conflict, the book argues for a move away from prehistory's conventional association with anthropology, historic battlefield archaeology's with military history and modern conflict study's with cultural resource management (CRM), to other connections that can be made. In particular, the long-term perspective on human violence and conflict that archaeology can provide is discussed in terms of its value to those disciplines that also seek to understand war and conflict rather than merely document it: especially but not exclusively Military Sociology, Strategic Studies and (especially Critical) Security Studies.

The book is divided into seven chapters that fall into three distinct sections.

- An Introduction and Chapter 1 provide the necessary background, explaining the reason for the book and outlining the need for it. In particular, Chapter 1 outlines the history and development of Conflict Archaeology – including its antecedents – and its current structure. Taking a critical stance, it outlines the 'fault-lines' that divide the periods of study, and the consequent gaps in coverage. The diversity of names that have been offered for the field is examined for their implications and the limitations they place upon its development.
- The three subsequent chapters each describe one of the three 'periods' into which the archaeological study of conflict is divided, emphasizing the distinctive qualities of each and the periods and areas each leaves unaddressed. The specific historical development of that branch of Conflict Archaeology are outlined. Key developments and texts are identified, and the specific discourse this encourages is analysed. The extra-disciplinary influences and links that exist, and the nature of the academic community thereby created, are made clear. Together, these chapters represent a comprehensive and challenging critique of Conflict Archaeology as it presently exists.
- Chapter 5 and the Conclusion look forward to what Conflict Archaeology could be and the wider contribution it could make to fields beyond archaeology. They focus on the dormant links between periods that are at present unexploited, and the benefits for the field of developing those linkages. They also look beyond

archaeology to the wider role such archaeologies can play in the understanding of human violence and conflict. These include the research, ethical and moral questions they raise and address; and the long-term global perspective that archaeology can contribute to other disciplinary approaches to similar issues.

The overall purpose of the book is to encourage proponents and practitioners of Conflict Archaeology to consider what it is *for* and how to develop it in the future. It serves as a 'call to arms' for those working in this area to consider how to co-operate more effectively with colleagues in other branches of the field and how to draw inspiration from each others' work. It also serves as an introduction to the field for students and others not yet involved, and will hopefully persuade them to take the field seriously and to inspire them to join it. Overall, it hopefully provides a model of what a fuller and more comprehensive future textbook on Conflict Archaeology may look like, and it therefore also looks to its own replacement.

1

Archaeology and conflict studies

According to John Schofield – a leading figure in the archaeology of the recent and contemporary past, and a driver of archaeological research into twentieth-century conflict: 'Archaeologists typically engage new periods by first examining evidence for warfare and conflict, taking note of military artefacts and architecture, before moving on to other themes and topics' (Schofield 2005, 13). This statement is in fact highly questionable; it is more likely that archaeologists first examine the monumental structures of any period, and as these may be robustly built of earth or stone in prominent places they invite comparison with the military structures of our own and more recent times. The result is – as for the Iron Age 'hillforts' of central and western Europe – an assumption of their function in war. More typical of the extension of archaeological concern to new periods, perhaps, is the capacity to take a more considered and sophisticated approach to the interpretation of such remains. An example would be of developments in the studies of medieval castles, no longer typically seen as built for war but as statements of power and status (Johnson 2002).

This book is about the rise of studies of war and conflict among archaeologists over the past two decades. It takes the position that there is a renewed interest in human violence among archaeologists that has developed over recent years and that this is both interesting and useful. However, while the interest in conflict covers the entire range of archaeological concern – the entire globe, and from the earliest periods of human existence to the present – it is in no way a unified concern but divided along period and geographical lines. The aim of this book is to explore the current state of this emergent Conflict Archaeology and to outline what a more unified approach may have to offer and how we may achieve it, building upon the achievements already made. These concerns – as outlined in the Preface – direct the structure of the work. This chapter gives an introductory broad overview of the field, offering initial justifications for the stance of the book towards Conflict Archaeology, including the various names that have been applied to it and what these indicate in terms of differing areas of interest among different archaeologists.

The emergence of Conflict Archaeology

Many will argue that after decades of silence on the topic, archaeologists rediscovered the human capacity for violence in the 1990s (Otto et al. 2006b, 14–15).

The middle years of that decade saw some key publications on pre- and proto-historic warfare in Europe and the Americas: Keeley's (1996) *War Before Civilisation*, my own *Material Harm* (Carman 1997b), Martin and Frayer's (1997) *Troubled Times,* closely followed by *Ancient Warfare* (Carman and Harding 2006a [originally published in 1999), *War and Society in the Ancient and Medieval Worlds* (Raaflaub and Rosenstein 1999), *Bronze Age Warfare* (Osgood et al. 2000) and *Deadly Landscapes* (Rice and LeBlanc 2001), among a host of other books and articles. Keeley's (1996) argument was that the prehistoric past had been 'pacified' by decades of anthropologists and archaeologists who had ignored the widespread evidence of violence and he sought to redress that balance. Although not all of the later publications were written in response to his charges (several had been envisaged before his book became available), he triggered a debate that is ongoing. In the decade before the publication of this book, a number of other major publications deriving from seminars and conferences in the area – largely inspired by attempts to respond to Keeley's (1996) challenge have been published (among them Arkush and Allen 2006a; Otto et al. 2006a).

The 1990s also saw a discovery of other classes of conflict-related object amenable to archaeological study. Work during the 1980s at the Little Bighorn site in the United States (Scott et al. 1989) provided archaeologists for the first time with a technique for the retrieval and analysis of the ephemeral remains of short-term instances of mass violence. Roughly contemporary and similar work at the Palo Alto battlefield site in Texas (Haecker and Mauck 1997) confirmed the value of archaeological work at such sites. The extent of the influence and inspiration offered by these experiments in battlefield archaeology only became evident at the first international conference on the topic held in Glasgow in 2000 (Freeman and Pollard 2001). Interest in the archaeology of battlefields has now grown to support a regular bi-annual conference deriving from the Glasgow initiative, the establishment in 2005 of a regular peer-reviewed journal (*Journal of Conflict Archaeology*) and battlefield research has been conducted in all parts of the United Kingdom, across Europe, in South America and in southern Africa (e.g. Pollard and Banks 2006a). The significance of battlefields as components of the archaeological resource has been recognized in the United States by the establishment of the American Battlefields Protection Program under the auspices of the US National Park Service, and initiatives in the United Kingdom, Ireland and on the European continent to establish national registers or inventories of important sites.

In Cape Town in 1999, the first international conference session dedicated to the archaeology of twentieth century conflict was held as part of that year's *World Archaeological Congress* (Schofield et al. 2002). Interest in the military remains of that period began earlier, however, especially with research by amateur enthusiasts into British 'pillboxes' from World War II (Wills 1985) and similar structures. The development of professional archaeological interest in the remains of World War I was particularly the result of road construction through Belgium in the 1990s, which cut through and followed the line of the Western Front. Excavations along the line of the road revealed not only extant structures – lines of trench, dugouts and strong-points – but also human remains from all the countries involved requiring repatriation and burial (Saunders 2001). Interest in World War II remains was inspired in particular by the discovery of just how much remains of the temporary structures that were built for particular purposes (e.g. Schofield 2001) as well as the interest in them evidenced by the *Defence of Britain* project, which, over the period 1995 to 2005, produced a database of Britain's surviving anti-invasion defences from 1940 to 1945 (Schofield et al. 2012, 109). The realization of the centrality of war to understanding the last 100 years led on to a concern with the relics of the Cold War (Schofield and Cockcroft 2007). Other aspects of the twentieth-century legacy of conflict – the Holocaust, the Northern Ireland Troubles, the 'dirty' and postcolonial wars of South America and Indo-China – have also become the subject of archaeological attention (Schofield et al. 2002; Schofield 2005).

One explanation for this explosion of interest in violence and conflict was the return to Europe of war, especially in countries recently freed from Soviet control such as the former Yugoslavia. There may be some merit in this: one survey of literature on this topic suggests that anthropological and archaeological interest in prehistoric war coincides with periods when wars are taking place (Carman 1997a). In this scheme, it was America's involvement in World War II that created the impetus for Turney-High's (1949) study of *Primitive War*, wars in Indo-China in the 1960s that led to Fried et al.'s (1968) anthropological collection on *War*, and US involvement in small-scale conflict in Latin America and the Caribbean that provided the context for Ferguson's (1984) *Warfare, Culture and Environment*, Haas' (1990) *Anthropology of War* and Ferguson and Whitehead's (1992) *War in the Tribal Zone*. In this scheme, the gaps between these publications represent periods lacking serious military action. On the other hand, a more recent survey of the literature designed to refute Keeley's (1996) claims of a 'pacified past' demonstrates continuing anthropological and archaeological interest in warfare from the 1960s onwards (Ferguson 2006). Ferguson is trained in the American tradition of anthropology, and for him archaeology is one of the sub-fields of that discipline: his interest is in extant traditional societies and the prehistoric past, which explains the lack of any reference in this survey to the much more recent rise of battlefield and twentieth-century conflict archaeologies.

Ferguson's (2006) survey emphasizes, however, the divisions that exist between these three periods of interest. The literature of prehistoric, proto-historic and early historic conflict rarely references that of later periods. The literature of historic battlefield archaeology – despite a current coverage from AD 9 to the late nineteenth century, a length of almost 2,000 years (Scott et al. 2007) and overlapping with the earlier and later periods – makes little or no reference to either prehistoric or twentieth-century conflict. The literature of twentieth-century conflict – despite frequently being led by those trained as prehistorians (Schofield 2005; Harrison and Schofield 2010) – makes little or no reference to either the literature of prehistoric warfare or to that of earlier historic periods. Although some students of prehistoric or twentieth-century conflict attend the bi-annual *Fields of Conflict* conference, these remain primarily the province of the historic battlefield archaeologist, while other conferences on archaeologies of conflict remain exclusively focused upon prehistory or the twentieth century. It is upon this division that the structure of this book is built in an effort to seek a way to overcome it for the benefit of all archaeological students of war and conflict.

What's in a name?

Although the term 'Conflict Archaeology' has been adopted for more than one university degree course in the United Kingdom, the title of the dedicated journal and as the sub-title for the leading conference series, it is not the only term that can be or has been applied to the emergent field. Indeed, the term really only came into currency after a discussion at the close of the Fourth *Fields of Conflict* conference in Leeds in 2006 where it was felt that the term 'Battlefield Archaeology' was too limited for a conference that also included discussion of prehistoric warfare, twentieth-century conflict, sieges and military encampments, among other matters. Nevertheless, the first such conferences – and similar events organized by the UK National Army Museum – described themselves as concerned with Battlefield Archaeology (Freeman and Pollard 2001; Scott et al. 2007) and this is a term still preferred by some for their own specialism (Geier and Potter 2001; Foard 2008). Indeed, at least in UK usage, the material evidences of battle that are the object of historic battlefield research are now called 'battle archaeology', a term derived from Battlefield Archaeology to distinguish these particular kinds of remains – which as will be discussed in Chapter 3 are of a distinctive nature – from other kinds of archaeological material (Foard 2008).

Others choose to call what they do by different names. Among them, perhaps, Schofield (2005) chose to call his book on twentieth-century conflict *Combat Archaeology*, but he does not justify the term and very little of the work recorded in the book is related to combat: instead it is structured and ordered according to a particular approach to the management of surviving structures as heritage (Schofield 2005, 9). Others who use the term 'Combat Archaeology' have a very different focus: as Molloy puts it, it is to 'elucidate ancient and medieval martial arts (and their social functions), the technological evolution of weaponry and the experience of the individual warrior or soldier from the perspective of the human body or mind in a combat environment' (www.combat-archaeology.org/index.html; Molloy 2007). For Molloy and his collaborators, the focus is on using material evidence – including the capacities of the human frame – to understand the experience of fighting in the past. For them, it is about the experience of immediate face-to-face combat rather than conflict, warfare or larger or more long-term phenomena.

As with any branch of archaeology, there are those who wish to further subdivide Conflict Archaeology by creating specific names for particular aspects. 'Military Archaeology' (e.g. the 'military archaeology and architecture' email list at militarch@jiscmail.ac.uk) tends to be limited to the archaeology of twentieth-century conflict, especially that of the two World Wars, and focuses almost entirely on military sites and material, avoiding civilian aspects, Holocaust remains and other types of evidence. 'Occupation Archaeology' by contrast focuses upon the material evidence of wartime occupation of civilian areas by a victorious enemy, especially the Channel Islands from 1941 to 1945 (Carr 2010, 2011). 'Holocaust Archaeology' (Sturdy Colls 2011) is – as its name implies – concerned with the archaeological study of landscapes of Nazi genocide and persecution during the mid-twentieth century. Similarly, there are a number of 'Archaeologies of ...' emergent in the field – among them, archaeologies of 'internment' (Myers and Moshenska 2011) concerned with various types of civilian and military imprisonment consequent upon conflict, and an archaeology of 'modern conflict' (Moshenska 2008) exclusively concerned with twentieth-century war. Others yet – although carrying out research that relates to violent events – prefer to eschew any direct connection with Conflict Archaeology and call it something else again, such as Saitta's (2007) 'archaeology of collective action', which deals with relations between capital and labour (much of it violent) in the United States. These namings are not in all cases intended to be divisive, and are frequently merely an attempt to distinguish one focus of attention from others, but together with the more overt attempts to separate particular areas of study from all others, they represent the centrifugal forces at work in any discipline, and especially any new area, as its practitioners seek to establish their reputations and their work as legitimate. The consequence, however – intended or not – is to further fragment the field of Conflict Archaeology.

Having said this, Conflict Archaeology is not without its problems as an overarching term. Like 'battlefield' or 'combat' archaeology, it emphasizes one particular aspect of the field of study. It is uncertain whether a person unacquainted with the wide range of objects that archaeologists of conflict address would assume from the name alone that it extends beyond battlefields and siege sites. To further complicate matters, not all may consider themselves part of archaeology *sensu strictu*: the work of Saunders (2004) and others may more properly fall within the anthropologically based field of Material Culture Studies. In practice, therefore, the wider field of Conflict Archaeology and its related areas address not only sites of direct combat (such as battlefields: e.g. Fiorato et al. 2000; Carman and Carman 2006; Foard 2007) but also issues of representation (Levitch 2004; Ferris 2006), memorialization (Black 2004; Kidd 2004; Trigg 2007), military encampments (McBride et al. 2000; Balicki 2000, 2007), military hospitals and their activities (Whitehorne et al. 2000; Reznick 2004), prisoner of war camps (Prentice and Prentice 2000; Doyle et al. 2007), the impact of conflict on civilian life (Shackel 2000; Johnson 2002), the development of military technologies (Smith 2000; Beck 2002), resistance to militarization (Schofield and Anderton 2000) and extra-military activity related to conflict (e.g. the manufacture of 'trench art', Saunders 2003; and art- and craft-work by prisoners of war, Becker 2004). In doing so, the field goes beyond a direct concern with the directly violent aspects of conflict not only to its more insidious but also positive impacts on society at large, and by taking such studies into the past, the field offers insights into how things came to be as they are that other studies do not provide. However, the full potential of the field has yet to be realized, as the divisions between its practitioners impede its development.

Conflict Archaeology and other disciplines

Conflict Archaeology has not emerged in a vacuum. Quite apart from its archaeological antecedents, the three main period divisions each derive from a background of research in other – albeit closely related – fields. Moreover, each period of Conflict Archaeology derives from a different field from the others, which perhaps goes some way to explain their separation. Not only are their origins based in different fields of enquiry and academic practice, but these also provide the intellectual agendas to which each responds. These too are each very different from one another. What follows is a brief introduction to this theme, to be more closely addressed for each period division in each of Chapters 2, 3 and 4.

Prehistory and anthropology

The study of prehistoric conflict is closely related – perhaps inevitably – to anthropological studies of war. In the north American tradition, archaeology is in any case a sub-field of the four-field discipline of anthropology (together with physical anthropology, cultural anthropology and linguistics): for that reason, publications in either field on early warfare will include both archaeological and anthropological perspectives, and the title may well reflect the inclusion of archaeology within the wider discipline of anthropology. In Europe, by contrast, the disciplines tend to be separated and so while archaeologists concern themselves with the deeper past, anthropologists study contemporary cultures. Nevertheless, the result in both instances is for anthropological understanding of the warfare of traditional small-scale societies to inform archaeological interpretation. As Otto (2006, 25) emphasizes, similar concerns have exercised anthropologists, primatologists and archaeologists in relation to the origins of human violence, especially that large-scale slaughter we call 'war', and each of these disciplines is equally divided upon the issue of the innateness of violence to humanity. Elsewhere, Carman and Harding (2006b, 3–6) focus upon the different definitions and conceptions of war derived from anthropology and how this influences archaeology. In contrast – but also reflecting Otto's interest in the origins question – Arkush and Allen (2006b) point to the joint interest of anthropologists and archaeologists in war as either a consequence of change or its cause. My own critique of the influence of anthropology on the study of war (Carman 1997a) emphasizes the focus of anthropologists on the institutional nature of war rather than its more material manifestations.

There remains one key difference between anthropological studies of war and archaeological approaches: while anthropologists can choose to study war as it happens, archaeologists are forced to consider the kinds of evidence left to them from the prehistoric past. Accordingly, for instance, Otto et al. (2006a) devote an entire section of their publication to material evidences, and Carman and Harding (2006b, 6–9) and Arkush and Allen (2006b, 6–9) both consider issues of archaeological methodology. Indeed, the issue of what constitutes evidence for warfare in the prehistoric past is central to its study: the usual reliance on human skeletal trauma, evidence of destruction and the presence or absence of weaponry or defences is highly unreliable (being themselves dependent on prior interpretation). Wileman's (2009) recent critique of this reliance is both timely and useful in its offering of an alternative perspective that sees warfare as a process rather than an event, taking advantage of archaeology's unique capacity to study larger processes over the long term.

Battlefield studies and military history

Critique of the close reliance of battlefield archaeology on military-historical agendas published elsewhere (Carman and Carman 2006, 16–19; 2007) have highlighted several factors. The study of battle has been, until the recent emergence of battlefield archaeology, the exclusive province of the military historian, and the traditions of this field have given rise to a very particular kind of discourse:

- a linear narrative of cause and effect, focused very strongly on the 'decisiveness' of a particular action, which can be understood in terms of the degree of effectiveness applied by the victorious commander in his use of resources;
- a highly functionalist interpretation, in which all the elements present in the story of the battle become assessed for their usefulness; and
- an approach, which, as a consequence, tends to ignore any interest in non-functional aspects of conflict, such as the sociology of military institutions, or any ritual or other cultural factors in understanding how conflicts come about and are structured.

Accordingly, battlefield and siege studies in historic periods focus very heavily upon weaponry and its use, the pattern of deposition of material across conflict sites and what this can tell us about movement through the space of conflict. It is an approach that is much closer to military history than the anthropological approaches applied in prehistoric studies (and has been defended as such: Foard 2006). It also seeks to explore sites of historical significance as defined on the basis of historical criteria – the presence of major historical figures, strategic or political importance, etc. – rather than those sought out on archaeological criteria (Carman 2005).

It is also a highly nationalistic enterprise. Although there is some effort at international research (Carman and Carman 2006; Pollard and Banks 2006b; Pollard 2007b), co-operation among particular individuals and some efforts at international comparison (Carman and Carman 2006; Pollard 2007a), in general the focus of such studies operates entirely at the national level: Americans' study sites where Americans fought, British study sites where British soldiers fought, Swedes' study sites where Swedes fought and Catalans study sites where Catalans fought (e.g. Geier and Potter 2000; Knarrström 2006; Foard 2008; Rubio 2008). At the same time, efforts to determine management strategies for this category of site are limited to the interior of individual countries, and even where cross-border co-operation is taking place (as between the nations of the British Isles), the focus remains on historically significant sites for those countries.

The consequence is a field dominated by historical considerations, generally ignoring the potentiality of other fields.

Twentieth-century conflict and heritage

The driver behind an archaeological concern with twentieth-century conflict – in contrast to both prehistoric warfare and historic battlefield studies – has largely been issues of heritage management. This is in particular reflected in Schofield's (2005) brief overview of the field, which is structured to follow 'a logical progression that conforms approximately to what is generally referred to in heritage management terms as the "management cycle"' (Schofield 2005, 9). In part, this reflects the other interests of so many students of twentieth-century conflict from an archaeological perspective: Schofield's other interests are in the field of heritage (see, e.g. Schofield 2008) and these are interests shared by others (e.g. Carman 2002a).

Although the origins of a concern for the recording and retrieval of remains from the wars of the last century lie with sometimes long-standing specialist amateur interest (e.g. Wills 1985), key anniversaries in the 1990s of both the First and Second

World Wars, plus the noted passing of the last survivors of the First World War Western Front, provoked a general concern for the material remains of these and other conflicts. The *Defence of Britain Project* launched by the Council for British Archaeology in 1995 (the fiftieth anniversary of the end of the Second World War) involved interested amateurs in the search for, and recording of, defence structures from the period 1939 to 1945. In turn, professional archaeologists found themselves involved in the recording of what was believed to be a small and diminishing part of the recent cultural heritage. In practice, however, it became clear just how much remains, either as unrecognized structures, as reused material or as interesting points of reference in the modern landscape (e.g. Schofield 2001). By the same token, since so many components of the Second World War heritage remained in use during the succeeding decades, such as airfields and military and naval establishments, the evidence of Cold War activity also came under scrutiny (Schofield and Cockroft 2007). In doing so, new techniques of heritage management, such as landscape characterization, were introduced to such locations and, especially as they went out of use, legal protective designations applied to them.

Interest in the First World War was particularly the result of road construction in Belgium, where the path of the proposed A19 motorway followed closely the line of the front line from 1915 to 1918. Rescue excavations carried out along the line of the road revealed extant and near-complete structures including dugouts, trenches and craters left by explosion, as well as human remains (Dewilde et al. 2004; Saunders 2001, 2004). In the end, the A19 project was abandoned due to growing pressure to prevent even more human remains being disturbed and to preserve this landscape of conflict, regarded as highly significant to an understanding of the last century and as a key material residue of phenomena that ultimately gave rise to the emergence of the European Union.

Nationalism

The close connection that exists between archaeology as a discipline and nationalist ideologies has been well documented and is now generally accepted (see, e.g. Kohl and Fawcett 1995; Atkinson et al. 1996; Diaz-Andreu and Champion 1996). Also, in practice, archaeology remains located within the boundaries of nation states, as national heritage agencies generally have responsibility for the remains within their territory, and this is recognized by international authorities who place that responsibility firmly on national governments (Carman 2002a; Messenger and Smith 2010). This, however, assumes that the archaeologies concerned are local or regional in scope: thematic archaeologies (such as Conflict Archaeology) are inevitably global in coverage since their topics are global in extent. And yet, Conflict Archaeologists – as has been mentioned above for those concerned with historic battlefields – remain quite closely tied to their own nations.

Although one might expect it to be different, this is evident even in prehistoric conflict studies. Despite the wide ranging titles of such books as *Material Harm* (Carman 1997b), *Ancient Warfare* (Carman and Harding 2006a), *The Archaeology of Warfare* (Arkush and Allen 2006a) and *Warfare and Society* (Otto et al. 2006a), all of which imply a wide geographical coverage, these collections – at least from an archaeological perspective – focus on the regional base of their editors. Of Carman's (1997b) nine case-study contributions, only two relate to areas beyond the borders of Europe and the Mediterranean; one of these is more properly ethnographic than archaeological. Carman and Harding (2006a) limit themselves almost entirely to Europe, with only one contribution from the United States: both editors are based in the United Kingdom. Of the ten case studies in Arkush and Allen (2006a), five relate to the Americas while four of the remainder cover the Pacific region; only one chapter is devoted to a region beyond this: both editors are based in California, a part of the United States on the Pacific rim. Otto et al. (2006a) can boast a wider coverage, but only by virtue of the inclusion of anthropological and modern studies of conflict: the purely archaeological studies are apart from one contribution entirely European in focus: the editors are all Scandinavian. The wider geographical focus in all these texts – which are generally illustrative of the approach to be expected – is supplied by anthropological material studying contemporary conflict among traditional societies located outside metropolitan centres.

A review of the publications coming out of the *Fields of Conflict* conferences since 2001 and the *Journal of Conflict Archaeology* (*JCA*) since 2005 tell a similar story for historic battlefield archaeology. Of the papers published in *JCA* from 2005 to 2011, the vast majority are by Europeans studying sites in their home country, with occasional papers by citizens of other territories studying conflict sites from theirs. While the study of prehistory is often based on one's own country, where conflict can be assumed to be largely local between adjacent or near communities, there is nevertheless significant international exchange in prehistoric studies and examples are rarely considered as representing an exclusively national or local phenomenon (see, e.g. Pearson and Thorpe 2005; Carman and Harding 2006a; Harding 2007). This contrasts with historic studies. The Kalkriese site in north Germany – location of the loss of Varus' Roman legions in AD 9 to German warriors – has excited international interest, but remains primarily a German focus of study (Rost 2007; and especially references in Wilbers-Rost 2007). Elsewhere, the focus is most frequently upon those conflicts that sit high in cultural memory – Jacobite rebellions against new rulers in Scotland (Pollard 2006, 2008b), Anglo-Irish conflict in Ireland (Shiels 2007), the Wars of the Roses and the Civil War in England (Sutherland and Holst 2005; Foard 2001, 2008), the Thirty Years War in Germany, and in the United States well-known conflicts with Native Americans (Scott et al. 1989), the War of Independence and especially the US Civil War (Geier and Potter 2000). This pattern continues into studies of the twentieth century: while British scholars are at work on World War I sites in Belgium, this work is limited to those areas where British soldiers fought (Saunders 2001); and while some show interest beyond their own immediate context (e.g. Christiansen 2002), most work on World War II sites is contained within national boundaries (e.g. Kauppi 2002; Schofield 2005; Foot 2004). This is true also of Cold War sites in general (Beck 2002; Dolff-Bonekämper 2002; Schofield 2004) but where post-World War II conflict study connects with issues of security and human rights, there is a wider geographical concern (e.g. Clark 2002; Crossland 2002; R. Saunders 2002).

Where studies of historic sites are carried out by non-citizens of the state where the site is located, there is nevertheless a national connection: usually the presence and active involvement of troops and possibly command by a nationally significant figure. The latter is certainly true of ongoing work at the Oudenaarde site in Belgium. As the location of a significant battle fought as part of a major pan-European struggle in the early eighteenth century, the site should perhaps be of interest to all those countries represented by the presence of troops, which include the Netherlands, the United Kingdom, France, Denmark and various states of Germany. The project is co-ordinated by a Flemish consortium, headed by the Ename Center whose base is across the river from the battlefield, and includes British and French advisors (Lachaert et al. 2008) but no other country has representatives involved. It makes sense for a Flemish group to lead since the battlefield is within their country, and the British and French interest reflects the fact that Britain and France supplied the opposing commanders. However, the historical consequences of the battle affected not only these three countries but contributed to the outcome of the war and thus to history of all of western Europe. The national concerns with the battle are not in themselves reprehensible – they cross territorial boundaries and reflect international co-operation – but they also indicate the kinds of interest generally applied: an interest in commanders and the immediate outcomes of battles rather than wider, less military-historical, issues. Despite the international nature of conflict – and the global coverage of Conflict Archaeology as a whole – it remains largely an essentially nationalist enterprise.

Critiquing Conflict Archaeology

The criticisms of Conflict Archaeology set out here – its division by period, its nationalist focus and attendant tendency towards fragmentation – provide the basis of the following discussions. By making clear the current weaknesses of the field, the aim is to highlight those areas that may deserve deeper consideration, but which may – by efforts to address them – also offer new opportunities for archaeologists interested in past conflict. The contention of this book is that Conflict Archaeology has something genuine to offer not only the wider world of archaeology, but also the wider world of scholarship in general – and beyond that the world of policy. But to achieve this we need to adopt the broader aims that a greater sense of unity can offer.

2

Prehistoric conflict

Keeley's (1996) *War Before Civilisation* argued for the 'pacification' of the prehistoric past by generations of anthropologists and archaeologists who refused to see the available indicators for violent conflict in the past. Instead, he argued, all such evidence had been interpreted as 'symbolic behaviour'. His book was part of an apparent revival of interest in warfare among archaeologists in the 1990s, which some have attributed to the return of war to the western political and moral agenda as outlined in Chapter 1. However, also as indicated in Chapter 1, Ferguson (2006) argues that there has been a continuous interest in war in archaeological and anthropological circles since at least the 1960s. From this perspective, Keeley's intervention can be read as an attempt to turn archaeological debate in a particular direction, rather than the reinvigoration of a defunct topic.

The nature of warfare

Despite the ongoing debates about the incidence of conflict in the distant past inspired by Keeley, there appears to be widespread agreement in current Anglophone archaeology as to the nature of war in that past. In general, it seems to be agreed that war in prehistory was different from the large-scale, highly organized and highly technological war of our own time. It is also agreed that there is a clear distinction between wars fought as part of a ritual tradition and the more rationally ordered wars of recent western history. In thinking of prehistoric and proto-historic warfare, we invoke images of restraint and of highly sanctioned controls on violence. However, as such warfare becomes something approaching our own style, the structure of societies themselves starts to change to something approaching our own: the loosely ordered 'band' or 'tribe' gives way increasingly to a 'state' type of society run by a military élite. War is thus considered to contribute to the processes of social and cultural change.

For Keeley:

> Primitive war was not a puerile or deficient form of warfare, but war reduced to its essentials: killing enemies with a minimum of risk, denying them the means of life via vandalism and theft ... terrorising them into either yielding territory or desisting from their encroachments and aggressions. . . It is [by contrast] civilised war that is stylised, ritualised and relatively less dangerous. When soldiers clash with warriors ..., it is precisely these 'decorative' civilised tactics and paraphernalia that must be abandoned. (Keeley 1996, 175)

Keeley draws very heavily on surveys of the anthropological literature to provide quantified cross-cultural comparisons which support his contention that 'The facts recovered ... indicate unequivocally that primitive and prehistoric warfare was just as terrible and effective as the historic and civilised version' (Keeley 1996, 174). Moreover, whereas 'the modern nation-state goes to war once in a generation, ... [and after adjusting for the duration of such wars, being] at war only about one year in every five ... 65 percent [of a sample of nonstate societies were] at war continuously' (Keeley 1996, 33). In addition, 'by the measure of ... mobilisation ... war is no less important to tribes than to nations' (Keeley 1996, 35–6). A valuable insight made by Keeley is that there is more to warfare than the formal battle. In a battle of warriors against other warriors formal limiting rules apply, 'but unrestricted warfare, without rules and aimed at annihilation, was practiced against outsiders' (Keeley 1996, 65). Here he turns the anthropological and archaeological focus away from mutually agreed modes of combat towards rather less honourable kinds: the raid, the ambush and particularly the massacre of non-combatants. Keeley finds all war – 'civilized', 'tribal', 'primitive' or 'prehistoric' – to be always total and unlimited war, in contrast to the common distinction between 'ritual' and 'non-ritual' war in the past, such as that proposed by Halsall (1989) for the warfare of Anglo-Saxon England.

In arguing his case for a warlike past, Keeley cites evidence from Europe and its environs to establish the prevalence of warfare in the millennia before literacy (Table 2.1). This tally of evidence of only 11 examples – especially sparse considering it covers some 30,000 years of human existence – includes two of the three main types of material generally accepted as evidence for warmaking in the prehistoric past. At Predmost, Gebel Sahar, Ofnet, Talheim, Fontbregoua, Hambledon Hill and Rouaix there is evidence for violence itself: the remains of human beings who show clear signs of physical harm by other human beings. At Darion, Oleye, Waremme, Hambledon Hill, Crickley Hill and Rouaix are sites which can be described as 'defensive' in nature: the presence of those killed by violence at Hambledon Hill and Rouaix, and of spent arrowheads at Crickley Hill, add to the likelihood that these were, indeed, sites intended for defence because they may have been attacked. Keeley's argument for the Belgian sites is less conclusive: the argument for the existence of a 'frontier' between foragers and farmers is a product of interpretation, not the result of evidence itself; and without the supporting evidence offered at other sites the possibility remains that the banks and ditches surrounding the enclosures may have been symbolic rather than functional. On the basis of this short list, Keeley attempts to persuade us that war was widespread in Europe before the Bronze Age and that it was as violent and unpleasant as any modern war.

Table 2.1 Evidence for prehistoric warfare in Europe (after Keeley 1996)

Period	Site	Description	Interpretation
Upper Palaeolithic	Predmost cemetery, Czech Republic	Mass burial with skulls damaged	War victims
	Gebel Sahar cemetery, Egypt	Mass burial with projectile points in or associated with skeletons	War victims
Mesolithic	Ofnet cave, Germany	Mass burial of adults and children with skulls damaged by axe blows	Massacre
Neolithic	Talheim, Germany	Linearbandkeramik mass grave of adults and children killed by axe blows to the head	Massacre
	Darion, Belgium	Fortified settlement on or near the frontier between forager and farming communities	Defensive site
	Oleye, Belgium	Fortified settlement on or near the frontier between forager and farming communities	Defensive site
	Waremme, Belgium	Fortified settlement on or near the frontier between forager and farming communities	Defensive site
	Fontbregoua Cave, Southern France	Early-mid Neolithic human bone deposits indicating cannibalism	War victims
	Hambledon Hill, England	Early Neolithic hilltop enclosure burnt; adults killed by arrows deposited in ditch	Raid
	Crickley Hill, England	Arrowheads in or near ditch and rampart	Raid
	Rouaix, France	Late Neolithic enclosure with skeletons buried simultaneously in ditch, most with projectile points in skeletons	Raid

Keeley's book is interesting as a study of prehistoric conflict in several ways. On the one hand, it tries to challenge the generally held notions of a relatively peaceful past as compared with our own time, and one where inter-community violence was limited. On the other, in doing so, it paradoxically works to confirm them. Throughout, Keeley is at pains to deny any possibility of a non-warlike interpretation of his evidence: explanations of bank-and-ditch enclosures (especially on hilltops), which rely upon their symbolic importance are denied in favour of defensive purpose (Keeley 1996, 55-8); the same applies to objects which he interprets as weapons (Keeley 1996, 19-20). Where a symbolic function is ascribed, it derives from the defensive purpose. The idea that such a site can be at once both functionally defensive and symbolic in purpose – or that the need to defend it derives from its ritual importance – is apparently unacceptable to him. It is in this style of argument that – perhaps despite his intention – the strict division between non-violent 'ritual' and the functional use of violence is maintained.

The nature of the evidence

Keeley specifically limits his discussion of the evidence for conflict to the ones usually encountered: defensive structures; human trauma; evidence of destruction; and weapon finds. It has been a standard trope of prehistoric warfare studies that the presence of war in a particular place at a particular time is signified by the presence of hilltop enclosures with external ditches, and of objects that can be identified as weapons. Finds of weapons in graves usually lead to the ascription of 'warrior' status to its inhabitant, especially in central and northern Europe (see e.g. Jørgensen 1999) and the identification of a number of such graves in close proximity inevitably leads to recognition of the site as a 'warrior cemetery'. The logic is clear but

Figure 2.1 Evidence of conflict in multiple periods? Dunnideer Hillfort, Aberdeenshire: crowned by a medieval tower. Photo by author

circular: if there are warriors, then there must be war; the evidence for this is the presence of all the tools of war; and the people associated with weapons must be warriors. The logic of associating walled or embanked enclosures within surrounding ditches with warfare is equally circular: if defences are needed, there must be a need for defence; the evidence of defence is walls and embankments; and such enclosures must be defensive (Figure 2.1). While the association of either defences or weapons with human trauma, destruction or both is quite compelling, and quite likely indicators of conflict of some kind, alone they may mean very little. As Bridgford (1997) has shown in her study of Bronze Age swords from Britain and Ireland, not all types show evidence of use: some appear to have been mainly ritual objects whose purpose was to be deposited as offerings, while others display signs of having been used against other objects.

In an alternative view that recognizes the inherent weakness of reliance on these uncertain indicators, which are capable of multiple interpretations, Wileman (2009) offers a longer term approach to identifying conflict. She instead seeks to identify warfare as a process that has antecedents and consequences, all of which she argues can be identified from the archaeological record. Accordingly (as indicated in Table 2.2), she draws on a wider body of evidence, some of which

Table 2.2 Archaeological correlates for prehistoric warfare

Wileman's phases of war	Correlates to be sought in each phase	
	Keeley 1996	Wileman 2009
Causes	Involvement in trade and marriage networks	Climatic deterioration Demographic change Subsistence or social threats Increase in social complexity Developing territoriality Changes in access to resources
Preparations	Appearance of fortifications Proliferation of weaponry	Appearance of fortifications Proliferation of weaponry Abandonment of settlements Appearance of defensible settlement strategies Changes in settlement location and/or morphology Change in subsistence patterns Change in trading patterns Unoccupied zones developing
Practice and its effects	Burned/destroyed sites Destroyed sites Human trauma	Burned/destroyed sites Unburied bodies and atypical burial Weapons trauma (human and animal) Weapons damage
Immediate outcomes		Changes in settlement location Changes in settlement morphology Artefactual and cultural change Change in trading patterns Changes in ritual and burial practices
Long-term results		Change in subsistence patterns Depopulation Changes in health profiles/standards of living Unoccupied zones developing Abandonment of developed arable land Changes in biodiversity

are those traditionally drawn upon, but she includes others that are more commonly left out of account. None of these is to be taken at face value: some are contradictory or may appear under more than one phase of her scheme. Rather, it is the accumulation of indicators that provides insight into the likely presence of conflict, into its form and its consequences for the communities involved and the wider environment. War is here seen as a process that takes place through extended time, rather than a single event or a series of single events: it is seen instead as a set of causes, choices and actions, the latter determined by cultural rather than any other factors. In this attitude to prehistoric warfare, there is a direct contrast to the largely functionally driven interpretation of later periods that are addressed in the next chapter.

Unlike Wileman's, Keeley's work does not advance chronologically beyond the Neolithic. Going beyond both Wileman and Keeley, Randsborg (1995) uses evidence of a boat and weapon 'sacrifice' from the Iron Age to explore the long-term development of warfare in Europe and its consequences for European culture. The site of the Hjortspring find – a bog, formerly a small lake, on the island of Åls in Denmark – was first excavated in the 1920s, revealing a buried boat or possible 'war canoe' in association with around 254 weapons plus other artefacts, some of them deliberately broken. Out of this 'sacrifice', Randsborg constructs his treatise on *Warfare and Sacrifice in Early Europe*, which he describes as '"not" a work on an archaeological find from Denmark in a European context [but] a study of ancient society, reflected in its material remains' (Randsborg 1995, 15).

The boat appears to have been able to carry up to 22 people, of whom 18 would be rowers, at high speed (Randsborg 1995, 23) and is dated to the late fourth-century BC (Randsborg 1995, 20). The numbers of spearheads, swords and shields found in association with the boat, however, suggest larger numbers: perhaps as many as five or six other boats were also involved with the crew of the 'sacrificed' craft, giving a total force of more than 100 warriors (Randsborg 1995, 38–42). The largest number of weapons in the hoard is spears rather than swords, together with numbers of shields and mailcoats, with bows and arrows entirely absent. Drawing on Roman writing on 'barbarian' fighting methods, Randsborg interprets the find as a post-battle sacrifice of the war matériel of a defeated invading force. Moreover, the presence of so many spears invites him to interpret this force as a hoplite-style army, fighting in infantry phalanx formation akin to that of contemporary Greece. Using the evidence of other contents of the hoard – a number of wooden 'pyxides' – he locates the possible origin of the invading force as Northern Germany (Randsborg 1995, 64–9). Here we see, then, an attack – probably a raid of some kind – by a 'limited elite' force from Germany on the coast at Åls, which was defeated by the local militia, probably fighting in a similar 'hoplite-style' manner (Randsborg 1995, 72). Randsborg is keen to maintain, however, a connection with ritual via 'a (probably mutual) code of combat' as evidenced by the lack of missile weapons, which 'stresses the ritual nature of combat of the age, perhaps even a kind of *rite de passage*' (Randsborg 1995, 54).

The 'sacrifice' itself, is of course, a ritual act, and Randsborg makes detailed connections between this kind of ritual deposit and other rituals in Central and Southern Europe (Randsborg 1995, 74–139). He goes on to make similar connections between developments in warfare in Southern and Central Europe and the North of Europe. In particular, he traces weapon development, from Neolithic battle-axes, maces and bow and arrow, through daggers to swords and spears – indicating a shift from non-specialized weapon and tool types to specialized weaponry (see Chapman 2006). Such changes in equipment, however, also indicate a shift from either 'long-distance' fighting by missile or close-quarter contact with axe and dagger in earlier periods, to 'middle range' fighting with long sword and spear in later times (Randsborg 1995, 146). These changes – or changes similar to them – appear to take place throughout Europe, either from North to South or South to North depending on the period, with new items also being introduced either into Southern or Central Europe from Asia. 'From about 1300 to the early first millennium BC, the weaponry in both the western part of the Near East, the Aegean and Central and Northern Europe, displays some remarkably similar elements' (Randsborg 1995, 164), comprising swords, shields and armour. It goes with the emergence of a 'new mobile light infantryman with standard equipment for middle-range fighting' (Randsborg 1995, 165) to be seen in the Aegean and Egypt as well as Central and Northern Europe: contemporary depictions always show such fighters with a spear as the dominant weapon, and this is reflected in grave-finds throughout Europe. For Randsborg this confirms the connection between the phalanx of Greece and the phalanx of Hjortspring.

The geographic link comes in the close connections of the Mediterranean to Central Europe, not only in matters of weaponry but also in the spread of religious and other ideas (Randsborg 1995, 201–10). While in Greece and Greek-influenced areas, the rise of the spear-armed hoplite goes hand in hand with the creation of the citizen of the independent city-state, in Central and Northern Europe the continuance of the sword 'should be seen in terms of élite or élite-sponsored warfare' (Randsborg 1995, 175). The real change to equipment – and full take-up of the spear as the dominant weapon – comes in the early Iron Age, and is inspired in part by the rise of the hoplite in Greece and in part by incursions of horsemen from the Eurasian steppes (Randsborg 1995, 177). Evidence from weapon graves attests to the shift towards the dominance of the spear as the weapon of choice in the Iron Age of Central Europe (Randsborg 1995, 178–184). Whether it also attests to a change in the structure of societies to a more 'egalitarian' form is not so certain, although

Randsborg suggests that the forces which began the process in Greece were also at work in the North (Randsborg 1995, 213). If so, 'this gives ... an idea of the powers of 'republican' ideas in Europe in the mid-first millennium BC' (Randsborg 1995, 184). It also provides a vital context for understanding the Hjortspring find, which is the result of Europe-wide social and technological changes:

> The society of the small Hjortspring phalanx, albeit in a context of military leadership ... linked up with a renewed ... outburst of egalitarian ideas, which in a great variety of forms have greatly influenced European society since the collapse of the Aegean Late Bronze Age. While the Mediterranean ... itself discarded many of these ideas for good, they were seemingly upheld in the North to a degree hardly surpassed in other regions. (Randsborg 1995, 217)

Discourses of prehistoric warfare

The hoplite-style warfare of Hjortspring appears to have had a short life. However, it does serve to exemplify some of the thinking current about prehistoric warfare, especially in Europe. Throughout Randsborg's wide-ranging analysis (in which he pays due tribute to military historian John Keegan: Randsborg 1995, 16), he seems happy that earlier forms of warfare contain elements of ritual, represented by limitations on the use of certain arms. The Hjortspring action is itself small-scale – perhaps involving no more than about 100 combatants on each side – and represents neither an attempt at full-scale conquest nor complete annihilation of the invading force, since at least some boats and crews appear to have escaped. In so far as it is recognizably similar to the warfare of our own age – in its organization and purpose – it derives from recognizable political impulses towards self-regulation and equality of treatment for all members of a given community. But the style of warfare represented at Hjortspring comes late in European prehistory, influenced by processes involving literate and therefore historical cultures well known to us. It therefore stands at the cusp between the familiar and the different. In such a view, all war is as much 'ritual' as it is 'real'.

It is interesting that there is so much fundamental agreement about the nature of warfare in the distant past. The writers considered here agree – one way or another – on the central point of warfare in prehistory: that it is – above all else – a cultural matter rather than a biological one. All writers agree that the style of a particular people's warmaking is determined not by factors external to them but by the workings of their own culture. In the case of Hjortspring, although the influence of other parts of Europe is strong, the hoplite style of battle arises not from environmental factors but is the result of cultural choice. The only area where there is some small element of dispute about the nature of prehistoric warfare is in considering the causes of war. For the majority of writers on Europe, these lie well inside the domain of culture: it is a learned 'habit' (Keegan 1993), the product of psycho-social forces related to prestige (Turney-High 1949), an integral element in all trade and marriage networks (Keeley 1996) or a ritual as part of a *rite de passage* (Randsborg 1995, 54). The alternative voice comes most frequently from across the Atlantic: Jonathan Haas (1990, 1999) urges instead environmental and demographic causes for prehistoric warfare, citing evidence in particular from the American South–West and East that during times of environmental hardship wars erupt and when these ease, they stop (Haas 1999). Rather earlier, Ferguson (1984) makes a specific link between warfare and environment in his edited volume. Both authors are keen, however, to point out, that warfare is a choice made by peoples, not an inevitability forced upon them by external forces over which they have no control. In American discourse too, then, warfare is considered first and foremost a cultural matter (Table 2.3).

Table 2.3 Determinants of the style of warfare versus causes of warfare in anthropological and archaeological literature

Causes of warfare	Determinants of style of warfare	
	Nature	Culture
Environmental		Ferguson 1984
		Haas 1999
Social		Turney-High 1949
		Keegan 1993
		Randsborg 1995
		Keeley 1996
		Wileman 2009

In part, this broad agreement derives from the nature of the community most interested in studying war and conflict in the distant past. Apart from the small number who come to it out of military history (e.g. Keegan 1993), most are primarily interested not in warfare as such but more generally in understanding prehistoric society. For them, warfare – its incidence, presence or absence, and its form – is merely one aspect of wider concerns that also include settlement forms, economic strategies, ritual life, intra- and inter-community relations, gender and a whole host of other matters that contribute to understanding culture as a whole. Very few prehistorians are attracted to conferences specifically devoted to the archaeology of conflict unless those conferences are also devoted to prehistory. By contrast with others who study conflict from an archaeological perspective, the closest links for prehistorians lie not with historians but with anthropologists and other students of human society.

This is nicely illustrated by a glance at recent key publications. It is perhaps not a surprise that a volume deriving from the US experience should combine archaeologists with anthropologists (Arkush and Allen 2006a) – indeed, in the North American tradition, Archaeology is part of the four-field discipline of anthropology (along with biological anthropology, cultural anthropology and linguistics).

Nevertheless the exclusion of scholars of war in contemporary and particularly historic periods from a volume that also investigates warfare in historic periods – African chiefdoms in contact with the Islamic and European worlds (Kusimba 2006), state development in China (Underhill 2006), Maori conflict with early European settlers (Allen 2006) – and whose authors draw inspiration from more recent conflict (Allen 2006, 185; Connell and Silverstein 2006) may be considered interesting. A wider range of contributors can be found in a volume of the same year from Denmark (Otto et al. 2006a), the 34 chapters of which are the product of discussions dominated equally not only by archaeologists and anthropologists (the latter both biological and social) but also by a number of other social and political scientists. The volume therefore studies warfare from the most ancient to the most modern times, allowing a broader consideration of human violence as a phenomenon, echoing the response taken by American scholars to the crisis of conscience caused by the Vietnam War (Fried et al. 1968).

The limitations of archaeological evidence inevitably have an effect on the way prehistoric warfare has been traditionally studied. As indicated above, the identification of the central European 'warrior grave' cemetery from the combined presence of a human skeleton with the remains of sword, spear, shield and other accoutrements (e.g. Jørgensen 1999) in a number of related graves has been a major feature of conferences on prehistory for decades. While more recent critiques of such studies – and others that identified female graves by the presence of jewellery and other 'feminine' artefacts – have done much to undermine a reliance on such evidence, the warrior remains a figure still sought in the study of prehistoric warfare. The reason for this is not, however, an explicit or deliberate search for warfare in the past, but an attempt to identify the different categories of person present in prehistoric societies. The warrior is one of those most easy to identify – highly gendered (most likely to be male, indeed at the extreme end of a scale of masculinity [Treherne 1995]) and associated with very particular and distinctive forms of material culture, especially weapons. Having identified the warrior as a distinct type of person, it becomes possible then to distinguish other non-warrior types, including males who do not exhibit warrior characteristics.

The focus on the study of prehistoric conflict as part (merely) of an attempt to understand humanity in its deepest past leads to an engagement with topics frequently excluded from the Conflict Archaeology of other periods. One is a closer concern with gender roles, and especially the role of conflict in the construction of masculinity. Vandkilde's (2006a) useful discussion of the topic emphasizes how the category 'warrior' is a product of various factors whereby a particular category of person – the warrior – becomes distinguished from others on the basis of age categories, personal qualities or status. The approach here is entirely archaeological – examining the material (and especially funereal) record of late Neolithic and early Bronze Age Europe, where among firmly sexed remains females tend to be accompanied by one set of grave goods, and males by others. This review of warriordom is supported by a further paper examining the world of Homer's Achaean heroes of the Trojan War (Vandkilde 2006b) in terms of status and gender roles. Such an approach is similar to the focus on gender taken by others, such as Treherne's (1995) discussion of masculine bodies in Bronze Age Europe and Shepherd's (1999) search for female warriors in Anglo-Saxon Britain, both of which rely heavily on evidence from burial contexts. Kristiansen's (1999) broader view of similar issues encompasses the development not only of material culture – the emergence and increase of recognizable weapons, an increase in concern for personal grooming (also identified by Treherne 1995) – but also new architectural and settlement forms to support an emerging, armed élite.

While such studies generally and inevitably focus on the presence of the more identifiable male warrior, they nevertheless – through absence – raise issues regarding the less visible categories of person they imply, especially the elderly, the female and the very young. A recent review of the literature by Gleeson (2011) argues that women and children are almost always portrayed as innocent victims who do not participate or take an active role in any kind of violence. Citing Keeley (1996), Vencl (1999) and Guilaine and Zammit (2005) among others as supporting evidence, she suggests that writers tend to make the assumption that women and children were the victims of prehistoric warfare, conflict and violence and not the active participants despite the evident difference of the distant past from our own age. Such questions do not tend to arise in the context of more recent warfare, where the category of 'soldier' is more readily taken for granted as a 'given' rather than an emergent social form. While a more detailed study of the place of non-adult non-males in prehistoric conflict waits to be made, the fact that such issues can be identified testifies to the wider range of interests reflected in the study of prehistoric conflict.

Conclusion

Prehistory reveals a wide range of topics open to enquiry that go beyond a mere concern with specific instances of violence.

Unlike those who work on later periods, prehistorians engage most readily with issues of 'origins' – of conflict in and between individuals and groups (e.g. Haas 1999; Otto et al. 2006a), of specialized tools for killing other humans (weapons) (e.g. Chapman 2006), and of the 'warrior' (Treherne 1995; Kristiansen 1999; Vandkilde 2006a,b). This places students of prehistoric conflict at the forefront of philosophical debates into the nature of human violence since the issue of identifying first occurrences beg questions of definition, such as what constitutes 'war' rather than 'warfare', and the difference between enclosures built for defence and for other purposes (Oosterbeek 1997; Kokkinidou and Nikolaidou 1997). They engage with issues concerning the evidentiary value of the mere presence of certain types of object in the archaeological record – such as whether swords indicate actual warfare, or represent an ideological tool designed to limit violence by placing restrictions on their carriage and use: such concerns have resonance in our own age of the 'deterrent' purpose of weapons of mass destruction.

Where questions of origin do not arise, the concern remains broader than a concern with issues of conflict alone. If warfare is one of the practices of a particular society, it raises questions about the manner in which it relates to other practices. One such issue is that of incidence: is it a permanent state of hostility to some designated 'others', a cyclical process, one limited to particular periods and targets (which may be internal as well as external), or occasional? The study of the type of mass violence engaged in – formal battle, the raid or the massacre (as at Crow Creek, Zimmerman 1997) – can reveal much about attitudes to others and social form. Where a more 'ordered' form of warfare appears to be the case, the study of the warrior as a particular category of person implies the existence of other categories of person just as important to an insight into how the society functions. The contexts within which conflict takes place – environmental (Ferguson 1984; Haas 1999) or cultural (Ferguson and Whitehead 1992) – may inform us of the triggers for a response involving mass violence, either locally to the society in question or more broadly to humanity in general.

Overall, studies of prehistoric warfare serve to emphasize the difference of the distant past from the present and to confirm the specificity of the emergence of modernity in Western Europe over the last few centuries. The connection with anthropology reminds us that most humans in most places and times have lived in small groups and that conflict for them is a more limited and more ritualized practice than we generally think of it to be in our historic past. The anthropological connection challenges the common approach to the study of violence in fields such as history, where modern practices and attitudes are so readily transferred to figures in the past and where contemporary attitudes go unchallenged. The study of prehistoric conflict offers a model for the study of war and conflict that allows us to 'stand back' from the concerns of our own age to think about it in new ways that can challenge our understanding of the world.

3

Battlefield archaeology

By contrast to work on warfare in prehistory, a dedicated archaeological approach to the study of the warfare of more recent history is a newer development, beginning with work at the Little Bighorn battlefield in the 1980s (Scott et al. 1989) where the methodology of using metal detectors to locate spent bullets was first used. Since then it has spread to the United Kingdom and mainland Europe, with some work in other parts of the globe. While the Battlefield Archaeology community is still quite small – large enough to fill a conference hall for three days, but small enough for the main practitioners to know each other by face and name – interest in the field has grown so it now can boast regular conference series and a dedicated journal, as well as more than one course of formal study in Higher Education institutions.

'Battlefield Archaeology' is a term used in two ways. In one – very specific sense – it is the application of particular techniques to study the material residues of past battles. As used in this sense, it focuses upon sites where armies came together to engage in a formalized style of fighting which was heavily rule-bound and sanctioned. Battlefield archaeology can therefore exclude sites of conflict between less organized bodies of armed people such as uprisings and revolts, sieges and smaller and more fluid military actions such as skirmishes. In a second, looser, sense it covers the archaeological study of all aspects of conflict from the most ancient to the most recent, regardless of period or style, and not limited to sites of violence but extending to military encampments and bases, issues of logistics, prisoner-of-war camps and the location and reburial of the dead from past wars. The currently preferred term for this wider concern is 'Conflict Archaeology', with 'Battlefield Archaeology' reserved for its more specific sense. This chapter is most closely concerned with the narrower sense, but its place in a wider interest in the evidence of conflict – a theme to be returned to in Chapter 5 – should be constantly borne in mind.

The archaeology of historic battlefields requires, as well as the usual skills of the archaeologist, a specific set of techniques and technology. While some battlefields will contain built features – trenches, walls, palisades, other earthworks, buildings and mass graves – to be surveyed, excavated and interpreted in accordance with standard archaeological practice, others do not. For these, the primary evidence will come from scatters of material left in the ploughsoil and found by metal detector (Figure 3.1). The evidence that is available will depend

Figure 3.1 Survey on the battlefield of Oudenaarde, September 2011. Photo by author

upon the period of the fight, the weapons used, the type of action – whether mainly infantry or mainly cavalry – and post-deposition factors that will determine survivability. As well as soil chemistry, overbuilding and changes in land-use, the effects of collecting and looting will have significant impacts upon the material.

A history of battlefield archaeology

While battles as events have been the focus of historical interest since the discipline of history was first invented, a specific interest in battlefields took longer to develop. Foard (1995, 343–82) records the early efforts of Edward Fitzgerald from 1842, whose work at Naseby in England includes the recording of field names and other topographical features, drawing the contemporary appearance of the landscape, noting where local people had found artefacts from the battle and recording where local tradition placed particular events of the battle. Fitzgerald's work went on to include the digging of test-pits and finding a mass grave (Foard 2001). About the same time, Richard Brooke was pursuing his interest in the battlefields of the Wars of the Roses, inspired in him by his birth near the site of the battle of Stoke. His *Visits to the Battlefields in England of the fifteenth century* (Brooke 1854) are largely discussions of the historical sources he drew upon and concern the events of the fight and the names of the prominent killed and wounded. He does, however, provide useful sketch maps of each site, some of which are of more practical use today than more modern ones.

Subsequent interest has largely remained in the realm of Brooke's primary concern, of identifying the places where battles took place, rather than using them as research objects in their own right. Once identified, the tendency is to assume that the landscape as seen today is similar – if not identical – to that on the day of the battle.

As Foard makes clear in his criticism of both the standard form of battlefield 'guide' and the English Heritage *Register* (1995), which so closely resembles such guides, most publications on battlefields continue to 'place stylised battle formations and key topographical features ... almost arbitrarily against a modern map base' (Foard 2001). Frequently, however, students of military history have taken the trouble to visit the sites of the battles they discuss and to relate the topography to contemporary accounts. Nevertheless, the primary focus has always been upon the literary evidence for battle action, rather than what the place itself could provide.

However, a group of unrelated twentieth-century researches moved closer to a direct concern with the battlefield itself, and while all have much to teach us in pursuing this field, only the last has led to the recent explosion of interest in battlefield archaeology. The first exercise in battlefield archaeology in the twentieth century took place in the late 1950s and early 1960s, when the then military government of Portugal sought – among other things – to celebrate Portugal's military past by promoting the deeds of its medieval chivalry. Excavations in advance of building a monument and a museum at the site of the battle of Aljubarotta, where Portugal first emerged as an independent state, revealed a mass grave and battlefield features (do Paço 1962, 1963). This exercise in battlefield archaeology has gone largely unnoticed by the battlefield archaeology community. A decade later in England, work at Marston Moor (Newman 1981) and roughly contemporary geological work at Maldon (Petty and Petty 1993) testify to the importance of topographical research and careful reconstruction of the historic landscape by revealing how accounts based upon the modern appearance can be highly misleading. At Marston Moor, the realization that the sunken road, which played such a large part in nineteenth- and twentieth-century accounts of the battle, was a feature added in the eighteenth century (and therefore was not present on the day of the battle) altered understanding of contemporary accounts. At Maldon, confirmation that a significant change in sea-level had occurred from the tenth century to the twentieth forced a reassessment of the one contemporary account of the battle; this in turn required the removal from the accepted story of the battle, several events which had been added later to allow the modern appearance of the site to fit the ancient account. The combination of careful recording of artefact scatters, topographic research and the search for remains of the dead at the Little Bighorn site in the United States (Scott et al. 1989) finally brought battlefield archaeology attention, and these techniques have since been applied in the United States at Palo Alto, Texas (Haecker and Mauck 1997), in the United Kingdom at Towton (Fiorato et al. 2000) and elsewhere (e.g. see Freeman and Pollard 2001; Doyle and Bennett 2002; Pollard and Banks 2006b; Scott et al. 2007). As a result of successful battlefield archaeology projects in a number of countries, the number of specialist battlefield archaeologists in Europe has grown over the years and the field is increasingly recognized as one of significance. The most recent *Fields of Conflict* conference – the leading conference in the field – held in Germany, had participants from 14 countries of Europe as well as the United States and Canada.

Methodologies

Practitioners of battlefield archaeology have in general been more concerned with issues of methodology than other aspects of the field. In part, this is because the techniques are still under development and – although there is general agreement on the approach to be taken – questions arise as to specifics. In part, it is because both the underlying purpose of battlefield archaeology and the underlying theory go unquestioned. The purpose is generally taken to be to provide an insight into past military practice, drawing on inspiration from military history. The theoretical approach, whether acknowledged or not, is an overtly processualist one, deriving directly from the search for 'patterns' evident at the work on the Little Bighorn. Despite the expressly anthropological concerns of that research, more recent attempts to incorporate anthropological theories of war into the field (e.g. Carman and Carman 2006) has generally been resisted.

The much-cited book *Archaeological Perspectives on the Battle of the Little Bighorn* (Scott et al. 1989) is largely the inspiration for the rise of battlefield archaeology over the past two decades. Taking advantage of the cutting of the grass at the Custer Memorial site, Scott and his colleagues used metal detectors to trace the fall of bullets and the ejection of cartridges across the space of the fight between units of the Seventh US Cavalry and Lakota and Cheyenne warriors. Differences in weapons used by one group of participants from those used by others allowed the researchers to identify Native American shot from that of the soldiers, and the distribution especially of cartridge cases across the space identified the movement of individual weapons – and therefore men and formations – through the space. From this, a model of the sequence of events emerged, which confirmed Native American accounts frequently dismissed. Other work on soldier burial sites allowed also the identification of individuals, the opportunity to infer the location of the bodies of missing soldiers and the chance to develop a picture of the 'typical' soldier for the late nineteenth century in North America. In particular, the researchers sought to identify the 'patterns' revealed by the distribution of bullets across the space: the 'static' pattern of the present distribution of bullets and casings; the 'dynamic' pattern of movement through space this represented; and from this the standardized 'post Civil War battlefield pattern' of military behaviour that would provide a model for interpreting other sites of the period.

A combination of discussions by Pratt (2007) and Sivilich (2007) allows an appreciation of the techniques of battlefield archaeology as they have developed since the 1980s. Pratt (2007, 6–9) outlines an effective survey technique by metal detector, whereby two operators survey an area, each using a different machine and at a 90° angle to one another, locating individual finds on a GPS recorder. As he puts it (Pratt 2007, 8), by using this survey technique 'coverage [of ground] is improved and typically result[s in an] increase of collected artifacts or more thoroughly substantiates the lack of metal remains'. Sivilich (2007) provides a useful survey of what can be learned from musket balls deposited on pre- to mid-nineteenth-century battlefield sites, which (because they are used in smooth-bored weapons and are lacking the distinctive features of rifle markings) cannot be associated with individual weapons. These include an idea of the type of weapon for which the ball was made, derived from its diameter and weight (Sivilich 2007, 86–7). Similarly, it is possible to identify whether it had been fired – from scorching and powder-burns on one side, and distinctive 'ring' around the centre caused by scraping along the inside of the gunbarrel; or dropped, by the continued presence of mould seams and sprues from manufacture. A scatter of fired bullets can be assumed to have been aimed at a target but to have missed it unless deformed, and to have travelled beyond it; whereas bullets fired and deformed may have hit the target but with insufficient force to cause harm: a combination of this information may indicate where the soldiers being fired at stood. A scatter of dropped bullets may indicate where firing soldiers stood. A particular development has been experimental work on firearms in order to ascertain what finds of shot on sites of battle may indicate. It is clear that fired bullets discovered by metal detector will mostly have failed to hit a target, but what is not immediately obvious is how far the bullet may have travelled beyond where any target was standing and how it may have been deflected by bouncing. Examples include work on case shot (Allsop and Foard 2007) and on eighteenth-century muskets in the United States (Roberts et al. 2008). Although not – as at Little Bighorn – indicating the movement of weapons and therefore individuals through the battlefield space, this kind of information can inform an understanding of the placement of troops during the action.

A central issue of the field remains the search for sites to investigate and their subsequent interpretation. Greene and Scott (2004) provide a model for identifying uncertain or unknown sites from the historic period, using research into the historical and other documentary records of an 1864 massacre of Native Americans at Sand Creek as a basis for archaeological survey of the identified site. As they put it, archaeology and history each develop

> independent lines of enquiry that are melded into a comprehensive and inclusive interpretation of past events. The Sand Creek Massacre Location Study is, in many ways, the epitome of such a multidisciplinary endeavour. [They then go on] In this case the 1997 archaeological study raised a number of questions that could only be effectively addressed by further historical research. The reanalysis of the historic record and the discovery of additional historical documents led to a new view regarding the location of the [site]. (Greene and Scott 2004, 63)

Here, as in the case of Palo Alto (Haecker and Mauck 1997), Naseby (Foard 1995) and Edgehill (Foard 2005), among others, the combination of historical and archaeological work resulted in a new understanding of a particular event in the past, one only available from the combination of different disciplinary approaches: this emphasizes that historic battlefield archaeology is inevitably a multidisciplinary field.

While historic battlefields from the seventeenth century onwards may be identified from historical sources, the precise location of battles from earlier historical periods are rarely known from written records, and much effort can be spent in locating them. The site of the late medieval battle of Towton in England caught the attention of archaeologists after the discovery of a mass grave close to the site of the battle (Fiorato et al. 2000). After its excavation and careful analysis of the human remains, interest turned to the fight itself and the search for other graves of those killed. Metal detector survey established that scatters of metal objects could be identified across the area of the battle, most of them attachments to clothing. Dense clusters were taken to indicate the locations of heaviest fighting. Similarly, concentrations of iron arrowheads also indicated particularly heavy exchanges. It is also likely – but has yet to be proved – that what these concentrations represent is the site of the pits into which those killed would be deposited (Sutherland 2007). Work continues to relate finds to the action of the day and to provide clearer insight into the military practice of the late medieval period (e.g. Sutherland 2009).

In more recent years, two battles from the Roman period have been securely located entirely by archaeological effort, both in northern Germany: Kalkriese, the site of the destruction of Varus' three legions in AD 9 (Rost 2007; Wilbers-Rost 2007) and a previously unknown action from the third-century AD at Harzhorn. In both cases, scatters of material brought archaeologists to the site and careful analysis of the distribution allowed an understanding of the fight to be constructed. At Kalkriese, excavations brought to light the barrier constructed by the Germans to prevent the escape of Roman troops into the surrounding country, thereby trapping them between attackers and swampy ground. Elsewhere, a combination of material scatters and close reading of the available textual evidence allowed the identification of the likely site of the eleventh-century AD battle of Fulford in England (Jones 2011). Close reading of topographic descriptions contained in the main contemporary texts allowed the identification of likely locations. Environmental and other survey then established the extent to which each of them might match the description given in those texts. Survey by metal detector then sought to locate the material evidence at each site that a battle of the period had taken place. What was found – rather than scatters of weaponry such as arrowheads, broken swords and spears – was intensive evidence of metal working, including artefacts such as anvils and other metal-working tools, the bases of hearths and incomplete and unfinished metal objects such as arrowheads. The much later battle of Bosworth was finally located only in 2009 after extensive topographical research supported by metal detector survey (Foard, pers. comm.). The identification of unknown or disputed sites has led battlefield archaeologists into periods otherwise little examined and where it is uncertain what material residues of conflict may be encountered. These 'signatures' (Sutherland and Holst 2005) are well known for battles of the seventeenth to nineteenth centuries where firearms predominate, but for earlier periods are less clear. The work at both Kalkriese (AD 9) and Fulford (1066) suggest that a key indicator of early battlesites may not be deposits of weapons, such as arrowheads, or of human remains, as at Towton (1461), but evidence of pre-battle metalworking. Foard (2008, 267) also notes the need to establish a 'signature' for later medieval battles.

A key methodology applied to the investigation of sites once found is that of 'historic terrain reconstruction' (Foard 2003, 2008, 26–7). This has been applied to good effect in the United States – especially at Palo Alto (Haecker and Mauck 1997) – and in England at Edgehill (Foard 2005) and at Sedgemoor (Foard 2003), where understanding changes in landscape type and use were crucial in placing troops in the battlefield space. Foard (2008, 26) outlines the stages as: a review of topographical detail from primary accounts of the battle; an assessment of the survival of documentary sources and physical evidence on the basis of which a reconstruction of the landscape at the time of the action can be undertaken; and a programme of archaeological survey to recreate an idea of the landscape at that date. Such a reconstruction proved invaluable in re-interpreting the seventeenth-century Battle of Edgehill, where traditional military accounts placed troops in a particular relation to one another that made no sense of the material recovered by metal detector survey. Historic terrain reconstruction allowed the identification of areas unsuited to particular types of troop formations typical for the period – especially infantry armed with pikes and muskets – and thus caused researchers to rethink the dispositions. Rotating the traditional alignment through 45° placed troops in ground more favourable to them and assisted in interpreting the archaeological evidence to allow a reconstruction of the events of the battle. In similar vein at Oudenaarde, work to reconstruct the historic terrain has focused attention on the area where enclosures met open fields, and it is here that the heaviest infantry fighting is expected, an assumption borne out at the time of writing by evidence from metal detector survey. In Foard's (2008) scheme, archaeology is used to support or deny hypotheses developed out of historic terrain reconstruction and the application of 'inherent military probability' based on a knowledge of military practice at the period in question.

The idea that sites have a distinct 'signature' is one applied by Sutherland and Holst (2005, 25–6). Although limited essentially to weapon types – and especially projectiles such as arrows, musket balls or rifle bullets – it can also include other material, such as clothing attachments on medieval sites where bullets are lacking (Sutherland and Holst 2005, 26). While Foard (2008) offers a clear methodological approach based primarily on pre-survey analysis, the discussion of methodology in Sutherland and Holst's (2005, 36) self-styled *Guide to the Archaeology of Conflict* is, although apparently more detailed in its listing, more limited and focuses on the search for artefacts and the discovery of mass graves. The differences are outlined in Table 3.1: Foard's initial methodological stages (numbered 1 and 2 for convenience) both correspond to Sutherland and Holst's (2005) stage 1, Foard's third stage of 'validation by archaeology' corresponds to their stage 2 and Foard's fourth stage of 'reassessment' of the written evidence in the light of both landscape reconstruction and archaeological survey corresponds to their fifth stage of 'proving' the site to be the conflict first envisaged. Key differences exist in the focus and purpose of historic terrain reconstruction, which for Foard (2008) is crucial and is both prior to and determinant of the archaeological research and its interpretation, but which for Sutherland and Holst (2005) is

Table 3.1 Methodologies of historic battlefield research

Sutherland and Holst 2005: Concise methodology	Foard 2008
1) Locate the approximate area of a former battle by analysing the geology, topography and road networks and comparing this information with historical descriptions of the site. 2) Locate and record diagnostic artefacts from the battle using field walking or metal detector surveys. 3) Collect more of these artefacts until patterns become apparent within the assemblage. 4) Once a pattern or an area of interest become apparent, attempt to understand the reason for this patterning by carrying out other types of survey. Analyse these patterns with a multidisciplinary array of archaeological techniques specifically designed to maximize the available data for the type of evidence already gathered. 5) Prove that the evidence is from the battle in question. 6) Once a battlefield has been identified, re-check the data with historical sources to tie the two types of information together.	1) Reconstruction of historic terrain from sources. 2) Placing events (and forces) within the historic terrain. 3) Validation of hypotheses using archaeology. 4) Reassessment.

simply to establish location. A further criticism that may be levelled at Sutherland and Holst is their evident belief that mere collecting of material will provide the 'patterning' they seek, and they make no mention of the need for systematic survey (as advocated by, e.g. Pratt 2007). However, in their defence, it is doubtful that they fundamentally disagree with Foard, and they are explicit in fully recognizing the need to relate historical sources and archaeological data. All these studies of historic battles share two characteristics: a derivation from 'processual' approaches to archaeological work; and a drive to contribute to the kind of understanding of past conflict that is offered by military historians. Mass graves represent a particular type of feature on which previous investigations have focused. The unexpected discovery in 1996 of a mass grave from the late medieval Battle of Towton required the development of a specialized technique of excavation and analysis in order to identify individuals whose remains were not clearly separable (Fiorato et al. 2000). At Kalkriese, investigators were surprised to find any osteological material because of the nature of the soil, but pits containing a mixture of human and animal bone suggested a clearance several years after the fight itself, allowing time for bodies of men and animals to be first looted and then left to decompose – thus denying Tacitus' claim of the construction of a burial mound (Wilbers-Rost 2007, 127–8). At the Little Bighorn site, work focused particularly on the identification of individuals – in some cases by name – in part to confirm the distribution of markers across the space of the fight but also as an essential component of reconstructing the events that led to the death of an entire command (Scott et al. 1989, 78–84). Very few mass graves have yet to be found on early modern sites, despite contemporary and antiquarian reports of their presence, and one reason may be that they have been sought in the wrong place: recent work by Bradley (forthcoming) suggests that in England in the seventeenth century the dead from the battles of the English Civil War were allocated to local parishes to dispose of, and would have been buried on parish boundaries within the battlefield space rather than the centre of the battlefield itself (*contra* Foard 2008, 52). The problem remains of how to identify the locations of mass graves – if any – from sites elsewhere.

There are two reasons for locating mass graves: one is to identify the area of fighting; the other is to locate human remains from the fight. In the absence of an ability to identify individuals, or even the territory from which soldiers originated, an important aspect of the work on human remains is to create an anthropological profile of soldiers at various periods in history. Here again, the Little Bighorn research led the way: the dead were investigated with the intention of creating such a profile for late nineteenth-century soldiers in the United States, and assuming the seventh cavalry to be reasonably typical, the average soldier of this period was young and poorly fed, although others were older and can assumed to have been seasoned campaigners (Scott et al. 1989, 248–52). The dead from Towton were quite different: there was a wider range of ages evident (Fiorato et al. 2000, 170), and several showed signs of healed trauma from previous encounters, including the man with the severe damage to his cheek and chin and whose face was famously reconstructed using forensic techniques. The kinds of weapon trauma identified at Towton (Fiorato et al. 2000, 172–81) were largely similar to those evident at other medieval battle sites, such as Wisby (Ingelmark 1939), Aljubarotta (Cunha and Silva 1997) and the otherwise unknown site at Sandbjerget (Bennike and Brade 1999). For later periods, a mass grave from Vilnius, Lithuania, found in 2001 (Signoli et al. 2004) contained the remains of nearly 300 soldiers of Napoleon's *Grande Armée* of 1812 and thereby provided valuable evidence for an assessment of the general health of soldiers at the time from the dental remains: results indicated that most were below 30 years of age and generally of good health; these findings matched expectations from the recruiting practices of the time, but said nothing about the specific social background of recruits since it was impossible to determine their countries or regions of origin (Palubeckaité et al. 2006).

Geographical and chronological focus

The problems of investigating medieval and earlier sites as outlined earlier in the case of Kalkriese and Bosworth are well recognized by battlefield archaeologists. It is therefore no surprise that the bulk of battlefield research focuses on later periods, where the location of actions is more firmly established. Such work covers the periods from the sixteenth to the nineteenth centuries, with clusters around certain periods within that time frame. Here, other questions dominate. In particular, in an effort to establish the value and legitimacy of battlefield research, effort has been spent in proving the techniques of battlefield archaeology to official agencies who are then encouraged to arrange for the preservation of key sites so that they will in turn become available for investigation and study. However, battlefield archaeology is no more than 15 years old in Europe and is still young as a specialized field. Techniques are increasingly well established, an increasing number of scholars are taking an interest and broader research questions – such as the development of gunpowder warfare from the fifteenth to seventeenth centuries – are emerging. Although a close-knit community of battlefield archaeologists has been formed, especially through the *Fields of Conflict* conferences from 2001, the largest impact of developments in the field has yet to be recognized, and the recognition by official agencies of the value of this kind of work has also yet to be achieved. Battlefield archaeology was until recently an entirely Anglophone field, limited to American, Irish and British archaeologists. However, it is now a global field with practitioners from all the inhabited continents.

North America

In the United States, much work focuses on battles from the nineteenth century. The work at the Little Bighorn site established the basic techniques of battlefield survey by metal detector and established the value of such an approach (Scott et al. 1989). Taking advantage of the cutting of the grass at the Custer Memorial site, Scott and his colleagues used metal detectors to trace the fall of bullets and the ejection of cartridges across the space of the fight between units of the Seventh US Cavalry and Lakota and Cheyenne warriors. Differences in weapons used by one group of participants from those used by others allowed the researchers to identify Native American shot from that of the soldiers, and the distribution across the space especially of cartridge cases with the distinctive marks left by individual weapons identified the movement of men and formations through the space. From this, a model of the sequence of events emerged, which confirmed Native American accounts frequently dismissed. Other work on soldier burial sites allowed also the identification of individuals, the opportunity to infer the location of the bodies of missing soldiers and the chance to develop a picture of the 'typical' soldier for the late nineteenth century in North America. About the same time, Haecker and Mauck (1997) were carrying out their work at the mid-nineteenth-century site of Palo Alto in Texas. Unlike Custer's Little Bighorn fight, Palo Alto was an American victory which had large numbers of survivors: whereas the former produced no eye-witness accounts, the latter caused participants to report on it to their superiors and to produce a series of drawn maps (Haecker 2001). It was these that allowed both the clear identification of the site and a focus on key locations, which would provide archaeological evidence for the precise events of the battle, confirming contemporary American accounts over the official accounts generally accepted since (Haecker 2001). Both these examples serve to emphasize the value of archaeology's contribution to the study of military action in the historic period, and also to emphasize the close relation of these to the precise concerns of conventional military history.

Such work has since expanded to the battles of the American Civil War (e.g. Geier and Potter 2000) and to other military actions against Native Americans (Greene and Scott 2004; Johnson 2007; Laumbach 2007). From earlier times, there is also growing interest in the earliest major confrontations between incoming Europeans and Native

Americans: the use of firearms against Native Mexicans at Peñol de Nochistlán (Haecker et al. 2007) may inform an understanding of the development of gunpowder warfare more generally.

Europe

In much of Europe, the focus lies upon earlier periods – especially the seventeenth and eighteenth centuries. The last battles in England and Scotland were fought in 1685 and 1746 respectively, and so British battlefield archaeology in particular has focused on these centuries. Foard has worked extensively on battlefields of this period, especially Naseby and Edgehill, both of the English Civil War of the mid-seventeenth century. Edgehill remains the only early modern battlefield to have been subject to total survey, following extensive historical and topographical research to reconstruct the seventeenth-century landscape. This, together with metal detector survey, established that the traditional accounts of the battle were seriously wrong in the way they positioned troops, affecting any understanding of the course of the action (Foard 2005). His work at Sedgemoor (Foard 2003) has further confirmed the value of historic terrain reconstruction in understanding troop dispositions and movement, and in locating specific areas for survey by metal detector for the residues of fighting. At Culloden in Scotland, survey in advance of the construction of a new visitor's centre soon established that the traditional accounts of the action and its limitation to certain ground only was incorrect (Pollard 2006). Elsewhere in Europe, research on battlefields of these periods has been carried out or is ongoing in Ireland at The Boyne (Brady et al. 2007) and Dundalk (Lenihan 2007), in Belgium at Oudenaarde (Carman 2012), in Germany at Lützen (Schürger pers. comm.), in the Czech Republic at Třebel (Matoušek 2006), in the Ukraine at Zboriv (Mandzy 2007), in Sweden at Landskrona (Knarrström 2006) and in Spain at Almenar and Talamanca (Rubio 2008), among others. These researches have in turn inspired work at nineteenth-century sites, such as in Germany at Idstedt, Grossbeeren and Lauenburg (Homann and Weise 2009), in Denmark at the Dybbøl (van der Schreik and van der Schreik 2011) and in Hungary at Komárom (Stencinger pers. comm.).

Beyond Europe

Although battlefield archaeology has yet to penetrate deep into territories beyond Europe and North America, there are some attempts to do so, although mostly led by European scholars. Work in the 1990s on the nineteenth-century fort at Eshowe, KwaMondi in South Africa was one of the inspirations for the first *Fields of Conflict* conference (Pollard 2001; Pollard and Banks 2006a) and there has been subsequent work at Isandhlwana from the same conflict (Pollard 2007a). Pollard also led preliminary surveys of nineteenth-century battlefields in Paraguay (Pollard 2007b). Landscape research on the sixth-century Battle of Dara has identified a likely location and features possibly associated with the action (Lillington-Martin 2007).

Conclusion

Battlefield archaeology is a new specialism that has yet to be fully incorporated into the global archaeology scheme, remains dominated by Anglophone practitioners and is driven largely by concerns deriving from a fairly traditional military history.

A listing of sites that have attracted archaeological attention indicates that the primary selection criterion is that of *historical* rather than *archaeological* significance: indeed, a comparison of the criteria generally used to select battlefield sites for archaeological research with those used more widely in archaeology shows this disparity of approach (Carman 2005). Battles are assessed for their 'decisiveness' against political or other criteria, and it is this capacity of military action to cause change, or at least to restrict options for action, that decides their historical significance. By comparison, archaeological sites are selected on the basis of their ability to answer questions about the past. The latter tend to be those that can be considered 'representative' of the archaeological record as a whole, while the former are always the historically distinctive and rare. This is one factor that marks battlefield archaeology as different from other branches of the field.

The focus is almost entirely upon the form of conflict under investigation rather than other aspects: whereas prehistoric studies focus also on ritual and symbolic aspects of warfare, and on the context for conflict, these are generally excluded from any consideration of later periods where warlike behaviour is deemed to be grounded in a functional rationality. Battlefield studies in historic periods focus upon weaponry and its use, the pattern of deposition of material across conflict sites, and what this can tell us about movement through the space of conflict. It is an approach that is closer to military history than anthropological approaches and has been defended as such: (Foard 2006).

The close concern of practitioners with methodologies of research – landscape research to identify locations, historic terrain reconstruction and effective metal-detector survey techniques – is indicative of its status as a new field. In particular, the emerging evidence that the 'signatures' of military action are different for different periods raises issues regarding the difference of appropriate methodologies for conflict in these different periods. The easy assumption that if bullet scatters mark gunpowder-era sites, then similar scatters of arrowheads and other projectiles mark sites of earlier conflict is challenged by the complexity of finds at Kalkriese and the lack of finds at Fulford other than evidence of metal-working. The straightforward transfer of method from one period to another becomes at least problematic, and this is further complicated if method does not easily transfer across territorial boundaries. Since historic maps differ from one country to another – and indeed may take a range of non-compatible forms within one country as a result of changes of rule – the process of historic terrain reconstruction becomes more difficult. To some extent this can be overcome by a focus on individual territories by citizens of those territories who are familiar with the methodologies required, but this raises the further issue of the highly nationalistic nature of battle research.

Although there is some effort at international research (Carman and Carman 2006) and co-operation among particular individuals (Carman 2012), in general the focus of such studies operates entirely at the national level: Americans study sites where Americans fought, British study sites where British soldiers fought, Swedes study sites where Swedes fought and Catalans study sites where Catalans fought (e.g. Geier and Potter 2000; Knarrström 2006; Foard 2008; Rubio 2008). At the same time, efforts to determine management strategies for this category of site are limited to the interior of individual countries, and even where cross-border co-operation is taking place (as between the nations of the British Isles), the focus remains on historically significant sites for those countries. There is some limited effort to internationalize interest in conflict sites but this remains limited.

If battlefield archaeology is to become a truly global field, then it needs the ready transfer of researchers from one area to another. If sites are, however, chosen for their historical significance, this will tend to confirm the significance of military historical approaches, which can be highly nationalistic. If the application of methodologies is determined by the specifics of national traditions, this too places a focus on research only into those battles of the researcher's own country. This national focus, although driven by understandable forces, thereby places limits on the ability of battlefield archaeology to contribute to a wider understanding of war in the past. Having said this, the emergence of research themes that operate at the cross-border level has the scope to both add to our understanding and internationalize the field. Such themes include, as Foard (2008, 267) notes, the origins of gunpowder warfare in Europe particularly in the fifteenth and sixteenth centuries, identifying the distinctive signatures of battles of different periods, and incorporating an archaeology of sieges into battlefield archaeology (see also Courtney 2001; Foard 2008, 146–80).

4

Modern conflict

Like the archaeology of battlefields, the archaeology of twentieth century and later conflict is a product of the 1990s and later. Unlike the archaeology of battlefields, however, it does not derive from the inspiration of particular methodologically innovative projects, but from concerns already well established within the archaeological discipline. It is also a particularly British phenomenon: while a concern for prehistoric warfare is evident across much of Europe, and battlefield archaeology first emerges in the United States, the development of the Conflict Archaeology of the modern era may have much to do with British obsessions with World War II (Schofield et al. 2012, 9).

The 1990s saw a growing recognition that archaeological approaches to the study of modern material can do more than merely help us interpret material from the past, by providing insights into our own culture that are otherwise obscure to us. This in turn contributed to a growing interest in studying 'the archaeology of us', especially in the United Kingdom (Graves Brown 2000; Buchli and Lucas 2001; Harrison and Schofield 2010). A more specific driver for the emergence of a Conflict Archaeology of the modern era, however, was a concern with preservation and management. As Schofield et al. make clear in their Introduction to the first collection devoted to the study of twentieth-century military remains, while such remains have:

historical and interpretative significance ..., in deciding which sites to retain for interpretation, which archives to present, there needs to be a more detached, objective assessment; there needs to be an understanding of what exists and what is important before such decisions can be taken. (Schofield et al. 2002a, 6)

Accordingly, surveys such as that of sites in southern England created to support the allied landings in France in 1944 have been carried out at the behest of English Heritage, the leading body for heritage management in England. The results were surprising, indicating the extent of survival of material and its ongoing use despite the assumption of its ephemeral and temporary nature (Schofield 2001). In the United States, meanwhile, archaeologists surveying for prehistoric and historic remains in the area of Nevada's nuclear testing ground could not resist also recording material traces of experimentation with atomic weapons from the 1940s onwards (Beck 2002, 67).

The discovery of previously unknown human remains from the area of the World War I Western Front in Flanders due to construction of a major new road contributed to the 'heritage' issues, driving the development of archaeological research. Here, the concerns were more overtly to do with issues of identification and repatriation (Dewilde et al. 2004; De Meyer and Pype 2007, 375–6), raising issues redolent of those connected to the archaeology of Indigenous peoples (e.g. Saunders 2001, 103) where questions arise as to the 'ownership' and proper treatment of the war dead. The survival of other remains from the conflict – dugouts, lines of trench, bomb and other craters, rear assembly and recreation areas – has also contributed to an expressly 'public' archaeology of the conflict (Price 2004). Particular public interest was aroused by the excavation of 21 bodies of French soldiers at Saint-Rémy-la-Calonne including that of the novelist Alain-Fournier (Adam 1991) and of 24 British soldiers apparently arranged in line of march at Le Point du Jour outside Arras (Sage and Evans 2001; Saunders 2001). Although – perhaps inevitably – dominated by issues of memorialization and remembrance, this aspect also involves tourism and the resolution of claims to ownership. As Price (2006) has argued in particular, the archaeology of the Western Front in France and Belgium can be considered an 'orphan heritage' since although related to people from all over the globe it is nevertheless located on the soil of particular countries who may not wish to recognize it.

The archaeology of modern conflict therefore raises complex issues of ethics, ownership and heritage that do not arise in relation to the earlier periods of human conflict (e.g. Wilson 2007; Moshenska 2008). At the same time, as Schofield (2005, 39–40) has argued in particular, the study of modern conflict constitutes a peculiar issue of chronology. The distinction between prehistoric and historical archaeology and the succession of one after the other is well rehearsed (e.g. Hicks and Beaudry 2006), but in the case of twentieth-century conflict this process becomes reversed: while the first part of the twentieth century can be considered 'historic' due to the existence of written material and oral testimony, the later decades constitute a form of 'prehistory' because of the secrecy rules surrounding the release of information. It is perhaps no coincidence that the leading proponents of modern Conflict Archaeology received their training as prehistorians rather than as historical archaeologists (Schofield 2005): this places their focus very firmly on the interpretation of material culture, a further distinction from historic battlefield archaeology.

The objects of Conflict Archaeology

While the central concerns of historic battlefield concern methodology, it is the range of objects of study that sets modern Conflict Archaeology apart. Schofield (2005, 41–80) conveniently lists these in terms of their physical form – as landscapes, buildings, monuments, cemeteries, vehicles and artefacts and artworks, as well as historical records. Particular foci of study include battlefields which may be studied in the same manner as not only those of earlier periods, but also much larger areas of fighting using the particular techniques of landscape archaeology, and beyond these to areas of civilian bombardment, military bases, training areas, zones of imprisonment and occupation, weapon testing areas and evidence for and of resistance to the militarization of society.

Battlefields

The study of modern battlefields has covered most of the wars of the twentieth century.

The First World War sites of Messines Ridge in Belgium and Gallipoli, Turkey, have been examined from the perspective of how physical geography, especially underlying geology, affects military practice by Doyle and his colleagues (Doyle et al. 2002b; Doyle and Bennett 2002). Excavations to reveal trenches and dugouts of the Western Front have taken place by volunteer groups at a number of sites since the early 1990s, including outside Ieper, on the Passchendaele battlefield, at Auchonvillers, France, at Vimy Ridge and at Beaumont Hamel (Saunders 2001, 103–6). Elsewhere, work has been conducted on the River Serre (Fraser and Brown 2007) and at Fromelles (Pollard et al. 2007; Whitford and Pollard 2009), both in France. The construction of an extension to the A19 motorway through Belgium provided both an opportunity and a reason to investigate World War I sites along its length, resulting in the detailed survey of nine areas including British and German trenches and dugouts (de Meyer and Pype 2007). Meanwhile, as part of a developing approach to World War I archaeology in Belgium, Stichelbaut (2005) was studying aerial photographs to identify lines of trench at a wider landscape scale. As de Meyer and Pype (2007, 378) point out, archaeological research can contribute to a deeper understanding of the experience of the conflict by revealing the contingent nature of military structures which change to meet new circumstances, thereby giving greater coherence and time-depth to historical sources concerning particular structures, and identifying otherwise unknown features and remains. Pollard and Banks (2007, xiii) supplement this by pointing out the valuable role played by archaeologists and others in identifying tunnels and other subterranean features that now constitute active threats to modern living by their collapse (Doyle et al. 2002a; Jacobs 2007). Beyond the confines of the Western Front, surveys of trench lines and other features have been carried out at the Finnish Civil War site of Ahvola (Seitsonen and Kunnas 2009).

In comparison with historic period battlefield archaeology, the metal detector is relatively little used in studying major twentieth-century battles. The sheer scale of the conflict, the amount of materiel and the extent of individual battlefields, discourages the use of metal detector survey (Pollard and Banks 2007, xi). Accordingly, traditional methods of survey and artefact collection from fieldwalking were used on the Pacific island of Saipan to identify the flow of action over part of the battlefield (Bulgrin 2006). However, metal-detector survey established a useful role at the Fromelles site (Pollard and Banks 2007, x–xi) by establishing the lack of interference at the site since the interment of British casualties immediately after the fighting. Metal detectors also have a recognized use on sites of the period outside the scale of the European Western Front, however, such as at the small skirmish at Kallaya Pit, Libya (Banks 2007), where the archaeology served to support the emerging historical knowledge which challenged accepted accounts, although as such it provided nothing inherently new. As Banks (2007, 27) puts it in summing up the results of the project, 'archaeological evidence [for battlefields] should never be divorced from the historical and socio-political context'. Metal detecting supported by the use of historical materials, survey and excavation played a large part in work on the Colorado coalfield 'war' of 1914, and echoing how the

Little Bighorn work supported Native American accounts, has served to challenge the accepted story of armed workers precipitating violence during an industrial dispute (Saitta et al. 2006; Saitta 2007). Similarly, although used by the Great Arab Revolt Project in Jordan (Saunders 2007) only as part of a wider range of techniques including archival research, fieldwalking, geophysical and measured ground survey as well as excavation and standing building survey, metal detecting has identified bullet scatters at the Jabal Abu al-Tyour group of trenches and the ruined fort at Wadi Rum (Faulkner et al. 2007).

World War I is high in European cultural memory – it is frequently (unfairly or otherwise) considered the classic 'pointless war' – and is of high public interest especially as we approach its centenary. However, other – less often recalled and more uncomfortable – wars of the century have also received archaeological attention. González-Ruibal, among others, seeks to relocate the Spanish Civil War in public memory. As he points out, at 'the peak of the war, the frontline occupied ... more than twice the length of the whole [First World War] Western Front [and] the remains of trenches and fortifications are astonishingly well preserved' (González-Ruibal 2007, 206). The fixed structures of the trench complexes of battles such as that of Jarama (Cobo et al. 2008) and Abánades (González-Ruibal 2011b) have therefore been subject to survey and excavation. Similar work has been undertaken at sites of the Second World War in Europe: especially at the Pointe-du-Hoc, location of a key moment of the invasion of France in June 1944 (Burt et al. 2007); and in the Ardennes, where a German breakthrough threatened the allied advance (Passmore and Harrison 2008). Christiansen (2002) identified the extensive remains of abandoned Japanese defences in the Marshall Islands of the Pacific Ocean, including stacks of live ammunition. Elsewhere, the focus has been more on presentation and public interpretation, reflecting the heritage concerns of modern Conflict Archaeology: such as the Dukla Pass, Slovakia (Leech 2002) and along the Salpa Line, Finland (Kauppi 2002).

Recognizing the distinctive qualities of the wars of the last century – their extension beyond habitable land and sea, into the air, into the civilian realm (Carman 2002b, 12) – a holistic approach that goes beyond battlefields is advocated by González-Ruibal (2007). Accordingly, the definition of battlefield has to be extended for any effective understanding to be reached. Work at Shooter's Hill, London sought to identify and record World War II remains related to the defence of London: these included a barrage-balloon tether, a pillbox, air raid shelters, a possible anti-tank gun emplacement and a mortar site (Wessex Archaeology 2007). In similar vein, Moshenska (2009) specifically advocates 'bombsite archaeology' as a means of accessing 'the immediacy of small views of everyday life annihilated by bombing: the debris of individuals, their homes and possessions' (Moshenska 2009, 53). As González-Ruibal emphasizes 'we cannot understand [Spanish Civil War] battlefields without exploring mass graves, military barracks, prisons and fascist architecture', concluding that '[i]n the era of Total War and of totalitarian regimes, it is totalities that have to be appraised' (González-Ruibal 2007, 221).

Military establishments

A distinctive focus of modern Conflict Archaeology is its move away from sites of combat to the logistical arrangements required for modern conflict. The publication of US Army Corps of Engineers *Guidelines for Identifying and Evaluating Historic Military Landscapes* (Loechl et al. 2009) serves to exemplify the rise in interest in the study and preservation of the built historic military environment and confirm its basis in heritage management concerns. In similar vein, in the United Kingdom and Europe, the focus is upon applying the principles of 'characterization' to such locales, identifying the distinctive features and areas that exemplify the essentially 'military' nature of the area as a whole (Schofield 2005, 128–30 and 149). Accordingly, both approaches draw on a range of sources – archives, aerial photographs, geographical information systems, building and landscape survey and oral history (Schofield 2005, 149; Loechl et al. 2009, 55–64 and 95–102). These are then used to develop an understanding of the site in terms of developing and changing land-use and site layout through time, how these represent continuing military traditions and reflect changes in military technology and mission, all giving valuable insights into the relations between the military and wider society. Such approaches have been applied in the United States to Washington Navy Yard (Washington DC), Edwards Air Force Base (California), Fort Sam Houston (Texas), Quantico Marine Corps Base (Virginia) (Loechl et al. 2009, 146–66) and Fort Hood (Texas) (Barrett et al. 2007) and in the United Kingdom, among other sites, to Bletchley Park Code and Cypher School (Lake et al. 2006; Monckton 2006), RAF Scampton (Talbot and Bradley 2006) and RAF Bicester (Lake 2002).

The 'Ocean Villas' Project in France (Price 2004) focuses especially on a staging area for troops on the World War I, immediately behind the contact zone of the front line; while the excavations revealed lines of communication trench, the more significant finds were of 'the debris of the range of activities that were carried out to support close combat' such as items of military 'kit' used on a day-to-day basis (Price 2004, 188–9). Schofield's (2001) survey of D-Day landing sites in southern England identified areas for the marshalling of troops, the preparation and storage of matériel, the harbouring of naval craft and the despatch of aircraft, as well as the necessary infrastructure for establishing and maintaining communications. Lake's (2002, 181–2) work at Bicester airfield and Talbot and Bradley's (2006) at Scampton illustrate the manner in which such places change as their purposes do but how past use and layout informs and is partly determinant of later forms, either by the addition of new structures and expansion of the site, or a 'collapse' to a surviving 'core' area, as required. Similar trends are visible in US sites as the varied needs of defending the newly established United States from external enemies, its expansion westwards and conflict with Indigenous populations, the emergence of new military technologies, involvement in distant wars and a new role as international 'policeman' required adaptation and development of military and naval bases (Loechl et al. 2009, 146–66). All such sites comprise not only overtly 'military' zones – hangars and technical areas, stores and administrative areas – but also 'civilian' zones including shops, housing and schools.

The impact of new technology is especially important in understanding modern military matters. Orford Ness in eastern England was the site of nineteenth and twentieth-century naval gunnery practice, was used for early experiments on military aircraft during and after World War I, and became a centre for military experimentation thereafter. In its latest transformation, it was the testing site for Britain's nuclear deterrent, its distinctive 'pagoda' structures (designed to collapse and seal in explosive and radioactive material in the event of a device failing a test) now dominating its landscape (Wainwright 1998; Wilson nd). Whorton's (2002) work on Cold War (1946–89) radar and missile detection systems brings to light an important aspect of late twentieth-century life: the inherent readiness of states both to go to war and the perceived threat of imminent (and sudden) attack that was symptomatic of the age. In an interesting counterpoint, Johnson's (2002) work on the (non-military and fragile) architectural response to the threat of nuclear annihilation challenges the focus on solid structures, while Beck's (2002) research at the US Nevada Nuclear testing ground indicates the role of structures designed to be short-lived and indeed set for destruction. More solid evidence of the perception of threat comes from recent work in Cuba, revealing the substantial preservation of evidence of Soviet nuclear missile sites from the crisis of 1962 (Burström et al. 2009, 2011). While these examples represent quite overt (and relatively hard to conceal) military edifices and activity, the more secret aspects of modern conflict have also become the topic of examination: the prime example is that of Bletchley Park House, home of Britain's code-breaking activity in World War II, the site of location of the German 'Enigma' coding machine captured by British forces and – in conjunction with the world's first analogue computer built for the purpose – where German U-Boat activity in the Atlantic was tracked by access to their own transmissions. Such was the secrecy attached to the work of the site as 'a global Signals Intelligence factory' (Monckton 2006, 294) that its architecture was designed to ensure the limited flow of information about activities both to the outside world and between sections within the facility (Monckton 2006).

Although the militarization of modern society has proved difficult to impede, it has nevertheless had its discontents; their activities too have been subject to archaeological analysis (although a colleague of mine who was involved in such activity has aired quite vocal distress at becoming an archaeological remain). The two exemplars of this come from opposite sides of the Atlantic: the archaeology of Greenham Common, United Kingdom, which housed nuclear-armed cruise missiles ensuring the United States a 'theatre first strike capability' in Europe; and the Peace Camp at the Nevada Testing Ground for nuclear weapons, United States. The archaeology of Cold War anti-military (and especially anti-nuclear) protest is argued to be 'unconventional [and] atypical, uncertain in its meaning, mysterious and disquieting ..., outlandish and unorthodox' (Schofield and Anderton 2000). The remains it records are those of temporary accommodation – tents, teepees and bivouacs; deliberate acts of destruction, such as fence-cutting; and the manufacture, construction and deposit of symbols of peace. At the Peace Camp in Nevada, a range of religious beliefs inspired a range of material responses including the construction of stone circles; stone formations were also used for more utilitarian purposes, such as hearths and way-markers (Schofield 2005, 100–1). In discussing these sites, Schofield (2005, 101) emphasizes the link between modern Conflict Archaeology and prehistory by dubbing the remains 'almost Mesolithic'.

Occupation and imprisonment

If civilians and non-combatants protested about war in the twentieth century, they also suffered its consequences. World War II saw the deliberate slaughter of millions at the hands of the Nazi regime in facilities built specifically for that purpose. Both World Wars (and others) also saw large areas of the globe occupied by foreign military forces both during and after the conflict. At the same time, soldiers spent years away from home, many of them as prisoners of war. These aspects have not gone unnoticed by archaeology, although they also illustrate the tendency of modern conflict archaeologists to create neologisms to distinguish what they do from the work of others. Accordingly, as well as Moshenska's (2009) 'bombsite archaeology' mentioned above, we have the phrase 'archaeologies of internment' to cover the investigation of sites where civilians have been held in a restricted space (Myers and Moshenska 2011), 'the archaeology of confinement' for imprisonment more generally (Casella 2007) and 'the archaeology of occupation' (Carr 2010) specifically for territories subject to foreign military rule during hostilities. The wartime disdain for civilian populations evidenced by these activities was not limited to combatant nations: as argued for work at the chemical munitions research and manufacturing facility at Parkgate, Dublin,

> the archaeological recording ... exposed an arrogance [on the part of the Irish government] when dealing with the legitimate concerns of the immediate population unwillingly exposed to the materiality of a conflict they had little part in [in the form of poisonous chemical residues]. (Myles 2011, 95)

While camps established by the Nazi regime in Eastern Europe for the mass-murder of Jews, Roma and others are the subject of growing archaeological attention (Myers 2008, 2011; Gilead 2009; Sturdy Colls 2011) (Figure 4.1), so too have other forms of civilian imprisonment received attention. These include arguably the world's first concentration camps in South Africa at the beginning of the twentieth century (Weiss 2011); World War II internment of suspect populations – Germans and others on the Isle of Man by British authorities (Mytum 2011), and Japanese in the United States (Farrell and Burton 2011); and the continuing use of such approaches by oppressive regimes in Spain from the Civil War onwards (Gonzáles-Ruibal 2011a) and the Soviet Union and its allies (Schofield and Cockroft 2011). Although focused on similar phenomena, much work on Nazi camps serves the primary interest of remembrance and treats the Holocaust as 'a past reality' that should be recorded and understood in its own right only (Gilead et al. 2009, 10). By contrast, a wider concern with internment across the century and into our own is designed to emphasize the process as one of 'social engineering – including ... the removal of a category of people from society to change the nature of that society' (Moshenska and Myers 2011, 11), either by simple extermination or using systems of control and 're-education' to transform attitudes. Such systems of control were also applied in Prisoner of War camps, and these too form one of the 'archaeologies of internment'. They are a particular feature of the two World Wars (although by no means unique to those conflicts). Investigations at the World War I camp at Quedlingburg, Germany (Demuth 2009), into the survival of World War II camps in England (Thomas 2003) and at Fort Hood, Texas, United States (Thomas 2011), as well as studies of portable objects from such contexts (e.g. Becker 2004), have provided valuable insights into the lifeways established by those incarcerated. By contrast, the rediscovery of the tunnel used by escapees from Stalag Luft III (the so-called Great Escape of 1944) is testimony to efforts of allied troops to resist imprisonment (Doyle et al. 2007). Meanwhile, recent archaeological work in a neutral country – Sweden – serves to remind us that the construction of camps was not

Figure 4.1 Auschwitz II – Birkenau: a site of internment and extermination. Photo by author

limited to the wartime period, but was required afterwards for those displaced by war and its aftermath (Persson 2011).

The internment of an entire population by the construction of a barrier across Germany as a result of Cold War hostility has led to an interest in the most-remembered portion – the Berlin Wall – since its fall (Dölff-Bonekämper 2002; Klausmeier and Schmidt 2006). Like interest in Nazi extermination facilities, the prime driver of this is the issue of remembrance and a concern to highlight the horrors committed in the names of 'state security'. It has its echoes elsewhere – the issue of security is at stake in the archaeology of the Spanish Civil War and its aftermath (Gonzáles-Ruibal 2011a), in the United Kingdom's Northern Ireland 'Troubles' from the 1960s (Jarman 2002) exemplified by work at Long Kesh/Maze prison (Purbrick 2006; 2011; McAtackney 2007), and in the study and preservation of sites associated with the Apartheid regime in South Africa such as Robben Island (Clark 2002; Corsane 2006) and District Six (Malan and Soudien 2002).

The missing dead

A focus on the battlefields and other sites of modern conflict often takes the form of the search for the war dead. The discovery of individuals from World War I along the line of the A19 road in Belgium – as mentioned above (Adam 1991; Sage and Evans 2001; Saunders 2002) – inspired public interest in the archaeological remains that lay along the route and confirm the significance of 'public archaeology' issues to modern Conflict Archaeology. A specific concern to retrieve American dead from the war of 1950 to 1953 drove work at the Hill 209 site in southern South Korea (Silverstein et al. 2007), and also in South-East Asia since the 1960s (Hoshower-Leppo 2002). As mentioned above, it has been a driving force for some work on Nazi death camps (Gilead et al. 2009). Elsewhere, the search for missing civilian dead of various counter-insurgency and 'dirty' wars (Crossland 2002; Jarvis 2002; Saunders 2002) provides work for archaeologists in South and Central America.

The search for the dead in these contexts is driven by the need to identify specific individuals and arrange their repatriation and reburial. In the case of war dead, the discovery of human remains will generally lead to an attempt at identification. In the case of the missing from other conflicts, the search will be to find the remains of individuals known or suspected to have been abducted, possibly imprisoned without trial or record, and killed. While Moshenska (2008, 168) has criticized much work on 'finding the fallen' as in reality 'finding the famous' – he cites the search for the remains of the playwright Lorca, murdered in the Spanish Civil War, the discovery of the remains of Alain-Fournier from World War I and the search for aviator Antoine de Saint-Exupéry from World War II – there is nevertheless a justification for this work. Especially for Americans, as those involved in such work point out (e.g. Hoshower-Leppo 2002, 80), the ideal of returning one's dead to be buried at home has been a part of the US policy since the mid-nineteenth century. It is a more recent phenomenon for British soldiers to be brought back to the United Kingdom for burial – the practice post-dates the Falklands Conflict of the early 1980s – but has been extended back in time for newer discoveries. Here, the role of the archaeologist is to advise and assist military authorities in the processes of identification and retrieval. This in turn raises other issues.

Discourses of modern Conflict Archaeology

At the Sixth *World Archaeological Congress* held in Dublin in 2008, a plenary session sought to untangle the emerging complexities of the relationships between archaeologists and current military practice, especially in the light of Western involvement in conflicts in Iraq and Afghanistan. In 2010, a WAC Intercongress in Vienna sought to further develop the discussion (Stone 2011). Issues that arose involved the ethical duties of archaeologists in the context of an ongoing conflict, especially one where the home state of the archaeologist was the initial aggressor, or at least responsible for the invasion of another's territory. While some argue for the ethical duty of the archaeologist towards the archaeological record and therefore a necessary collaboration with the military to ensure the protection of important sites and remains (Curtis 2009; Stone 2011), others take the line that opposition to war in one's capacity as a citizen must mean non-engagement with the military, even at the cost of the loss of important remains (Hamilakis 2003, 2009). It is not the place or purpose of this book to rehearse these arguments in any detail, but it is a further indication of the difference of modern Conflict Archaeology from that of earlier periods. Neither the prehistorian nor the historic battlefield archaeologist need feel any direct engagement with their object of study: they bear no particular moral responsibility except as regards the proper treatment of archaeological material in accordance with professional practice.

Unlike prehistoric and historic conflict, modern conflict did not stop with the two World Wars or the Cold War and its immediate offshoots in Korea, Vietnam and the 'dirty wars' of Latin America and Africa, among others. It leaves its legacy in more recent hostilities in the Balkans and the former Soviet Union, and in the post-colonial context across the globe. Further wars proliferate as new threats are identified and challenged, and rumours of wars to come are the stuff of journalistic commentary. While archaeologists may study the conflicts of the twentieth century as 'past' – even those within living memory – they nonetheless raise important issues concerning what is appropriate to study and how. Brown outlines his role in working with the British military as a concern for the 'heritage' writ broadly, including that of the military themselves, and an appreciation of different attitudes held by archaeologists and soldiers 'can be used advantageously as part of the process of heritage protection [to] engender a more positive environment for messages about protection of cultural property overseas' (Brown 2011, 136). However, modern conflicts also have ongoing consequences for people other than archaeologists: while none are left who directly experienced the World War I Western Front, their near relatives survive and the memory of later conflicts is still real for their participants. Every day new casualties from conflicts in Iraq and Afghanistan are returned home (as I write, a helicopter carrying wounded is flying overhead to deposit its cargo to the Queen Elizabeth Hospital in Birmingham) and new memorials are raised to those who have served. An archaeology of modern conflict has inevitably also to engage with the ongoing nature of conflict.

While arguments take place among archaeologists on these issues, modern Conflict Archaeology generally remains detached from other branches of Conflict Archaeology. Some attend the *Fields of Conflict* conference series but relatively few: and at the sixth such conference in Osnabrück they were separated out into their own session held in parallel with another focused on historic battles. Instead, conferences and sessions devoted to modern conflict are held independently and few engaged in other aspects of conflict attend. Like the prehistory of conflict and battlefield archaeology, modern conflict is a relatively enclosed self-referencing world.

Conclusion

The modern period is one where it can be argued that war and rumour of war has dominated life. The devastating wars of the twentieth century are the key moments that determine historical understanding; the twentieth century can be claimed to have really begun in 1914 with the outbreak of a general European conflict, to reach its midpoint in 1945 with the end of another and a global political reorientation that determined things until 1989, at which point we enter the world of our own century with its confusion of polities and interventions.

Archaeologists are used to dealing with time on the large scale (Bailey 1983; Murray 1999): prehistory is long, historic time shorter and our own age remarkably short by comparison. It is perhaps the immediacy of modern conflict that encourages the division of its study into separate departments: the series of 'archaeologies of ...' bombing, internment, occupation and warfare noted above; it is a way of engaging with the 'speeding up' of time that our age encourages. This does also, however, encourage a separation of particular aspects of modern conflict from one another: the fighting of armies in World War II, for instance, becomes separated from a consideration of the bombing of civilian targets, of the occupation of otherwise neutral populations, of the militarization of land otherwise untouched by war and of the imprisonment and industrialized mass murder of individuals selected by imposed categories. The crossing of boundaries does in some measure overcome these divisions – the combined study of Cold War military sites with evidence of anti-war resistance at or adjacent to those sites, for instance. However, the practice of division raises the threat of separation that disallows a true appreciation of how military activity in the twentieth century and later has impacted more generally on society.

On the other hand, the range of objects of study identified by modern Conflict Archaeology offers a distinctive view of the way violence on the large scale – actual or threatened – affects landscapes, building styles, societies and the human environment more generally. An appreciation of their interaction is crucial to understanding the development of modern conflict, where the focus of activity is increasingly removed from the formal military to the civilian realm. This in turn refers to the ethical issues that arise. These include not only archaeologists' relations with current military activity to protect cultural property, but also how we engage with those who make an emotional claim to the conflicts, material and events under study. As Moshenska (2008) makes clear, these relate to other ethical issues identified in archaeology, such as engagements with communities and human remains, so are not entirely unique to modern Conflict Archaeology. However, such is the emotional power of engagement with conflict that these issues gain a particular significance. The potential of modern Conflict Archaeology to inform us of our own attitudes to our own period of history is therefore not to be underestimated. At the same time, by raising ethical issues concerning archaeological relations to the military, modern Conflict Archaeology provides a locale for wider debates about the role of the military and of military action – indeed of violence more generally.

5

The potential of Conflict Archaeology

It will have been evident from Chapters 2, 3 and 4 that there are noticeable gaps in the coverage of Conflict Archaeology as it has developed in the past decades. In particular, while a concern for European and North American prehistoric conflict is evident, this largely does not extend to other parts of the globe except in terms of the search for ethnographic examples. Similarly, while prehistoric interest ceases with the rise of literate cultures, and apart from one or two notable exceptions, concern for historic periods really only begins with the later European Middle Ages. This is partly explicable by the focus by students of Classical Greek and Roman warfare on written texts as the source (e.g. for ancient Greek warfare, Hanson 1989) and more explicitly archaeological or landscape approaches generally limited to decades prior to the emergence of Conflict Archaeology as a distinct field (see e.g. Pritchett 1957, 1958).

Other more recent historic periods also suffer from a lack of explicit focus. The sixteenth century in Europe, although a period that may be considered significant in terms of a shift of warfare style from 'shock' to gunpowder and the commencement of Europe's global expansion as a colonizing force, is relatively untouched apart from studies of fortifications or shipping. The late nineteenth century is also low in coverage, except for North American conflict with Native Americans: this may partly be explained by the generally successful exportation of warfare by the major European states to colonial contexts from the close of the Napoleonic Wars to 1914. There are some exceptions to this general rule such as the Crimean War, the Franco-Austrian and Franco-Prussian Wars and the wars of German and other national unifications from mid-century, although these too remain largely unexamined from an archaeological perspective. Consequently, there is a chronological leap from the eighteenth century to the twentieth century, the latter forming an entirely separate area of study from that of the historic period.

In part, these lacunae can be explained by the relative newness of the field and the small number of practitioners: no one can do everything, and it does no one any good to attempt a rushed approach. However, they also derive from the kinds of concerns that drive the main branches of Conflict Archaeology as it has developed and the separation of chronological periods in terms of methodologies and purpose.

Developments which are beginning to emerge include the recognition that the archaeology of periods beyond those of the historic may have things to contribute to the study of historic battlefields. These reflect in large measure the wider range of interests evident in modern Conflict Archaeology, but there are also hints at ways to exploit the insights of prehistoric study.

Beyond the bounds of historic battlefield archaeology

Fortifications and other structures

Alongside the developing interest in battlesites, there has also been a growing concern for other sites of conflict-related activity. The most obvious of these are the sites of fortifications (Figure 5.1) of various kinds, addressed especially for the United Kingdom by Coad (2005) in a review paper given to the UK-based Society for Post-Medieval

Figure 5.1 Fortress, trading post and residence: the 'French Castle' (seventeenth century), Old Fort Niagara, New York, United States. Photo by author

Archaeology. The Society's journal has since published several papers on precisely the topic of fortifications. Investigations at Landguard Fort, Harwich (Meredith et al. 2008), as well as providing the first sizeable assemblage of late seventeenth-century clay pipes from the region, focused on the relation of construction to known military threats. A similar focus was evident on work over more than a decade at Fort George, near Inverness in Scotland (Ewart and Gallagher 2010). Excavations in Quebec, Canada, from 2005 exposed evidence of fortification by early settlers initially for defence against and as a base from which to engage with local Indigenous peoples, and later for conflict with other colonizing Europeans (Cloutier and L'Anglais 2009; Fiset and Samson 2009; Guimont 2009). At Fort Beauséjour – Fort Cumberland, Canada, a siege trench and related blockhouse from 1755 was firmly located using LiDAR, confirming its survival as a low-resolution feature and its relationship to contemporary plans (Millard et al. 2009). Elsewhere, a more landscape-focused approach has been taken. Survey of the eighteenth- and nineteenth-century defences around Keesi, Yorubaland, Nigeria, indicated their combined use with thick forest to deter attack from neighbouring groups, reducing reliance on a total enclosure by ramparts and ditches (Odunbaku and Alabi 2010), a direct contrast with European traditions. In Portugal, study of sixteenth- and seventeenth-century forts on the Arrábida coast relates their construction, modification and – crucially – naming and architectural style to issues of the increasing power and centralizing control of the Portuguese crown (Portocarrero 2011). In similar vein, the defences of Sydney's harbour in Australia provides for Gojak (2002, 169) 'a detailed reflection of the shifting relationship between an increasingly independent [Australia] and its 'mother' Britain, and the economically dominant United States'.

A contrasting object from those structures built by military engineers are those structures occupied by civilian populations. These include fortified churches which are present in Ireland (Doran 2007), but are also widespread through borderlands in Europe and both fortified churches and subterranean villages in northern France (Derwerdt and Willmann 2003) (Figure 5.2). These, together with Grguric's (2008) study of fortified homesteads in late-nineteenth-century Australia confirm the important role of fear in the construction and maintenance of certain kinds of material culture. In similar vein, the fortifications of Europe's walled cities have been examined to consider not only their form and extent, but also 'their relationship with the urban context, their effects as barriers within the townscape [and their use and exploitation] by different groups over the centuries' (Bruce and Creighton 2006, 249). Frazer's (2007) research into Irish cottier settlement of the sixteenth to seventeenth centuries suggests material culture evidence apart from bullets and weapon-parts (such as the many keys found) may be used to infer 'troublous times', while certain changes in landscape use and crop production may be interpreted as a response to uncertainty. Useful studies of civilian reaction to American Civil War activity (farming on the Antietam battlefield: Manning-Sterling

Figure 5.2 Fortified church at Scy-Chazelles, Metz, France. 'Home' church of Robert Schuman, Mayor of Metz and co-founder of the European Union. Photo by author

2000; ongoing occupation of the Robinson home at Manassas: Seibert and Parsons 2000; and urban life in Harper's Ferry, Virginia: Shackel 2000) provide further insight into the development of civilian–military relations, and their division into separate social realms, as we approach closer to our own time. Such studies take us beyond the conventional concerns of Conflict Archaeology 'proper' by a direct engagement of the meanings of place beyond that of purely military use. These concerns are perhaps no less to do with conflict in its wider sense than specific sites of war, although focused more on the intra-societal relations between categories of persons than inter-societal differences.

Military infrastructure and logistics

Studies of armies of the major ancient civilizations from an archaeological perspective are relatively rare. Where they do occur, the focus is much more on logistical and organizational factors than as fighting machines even though this does underpin the interest (see, e.g. on the Roman army, Thomas and Stallibrass 2008; Goldsworthy and Adams 1999). The potential of archaeology to contribute to an understanding of military logistics and how large numbers of men, animals and transports could be delivered across large distances to engage an enemy is, however, being explored in the Medieval Warfare on the GRID project led out of Birmingham University. This attempts to model the movement of the Byzantine army to its defeat at Manzikert in 1071 (Haldon 2006, 8–18; Gaffney et al. forthcoming), examining in particular the routes through Asia Minor available to provide access, food and fodder. Although primarily an exercise in digital modelling, it relies upon the archaeological reconstruction of landscape and environment to allow interpretation.

As historic warfare transforms into modern conflict, the need for logistical support grows. This is highly evident in America's Civil War, where several of the features of modern military organization have been subject to investigation. Balicki (2007) studied the Confederate cantonment at Evansport, Virginia, emphasizing its location in relation to purely military factors, allowing effective blockade of the Potomac River and protection from enemy bombardment, but also thereby denying troops such amenities as 'exposure to winter sunlight and being out of the wind' (Balicki 2007, 274): here is an example of the clear separation of military convenience from soldierly comfort. Research at the site of Fort Nelson, Kentucky emphasizes how 'military depots of the [American] Civil War were complex settlements' comprising both civilian and military elements (McBride et al. 2000). The massive numbers of casualties from the war placed great strains on medical facilities, but by the later years of the war effective systems for the treatment of casualties were put in place, as evidenced by the discovery of the 1864 field hospital at Winchester, Virginia (Whitehorne et al. 2000). Elsewhere, things were worse, as at Andersonville Prison for prisoners of war, which displays many of the features associated with twentieth-century camps, including an interior 'deadline' (the crossing of which was forbidden) and tunnels for attempted escape (Prentice and Prentice 2000).

Disciplinary cross-connections

Research in earlier periods into the aspects of military life most evident in the modern period provide an opportunity to identify the moments when the distinctive characteristics of modern conflict emerged. As Saunders (2004, 5) puts it, modern war 'simultaneously creates and destroys more than any previous kind of conflict' and can therefore be considered unique, justifying its separation from other eras. However, many of the features of modern conflict are not in themselves new: non-combatant casualties are as evident in past centuries as in our own, defensive structures have a deep history and the effects of emerging technologies can be identified in prehistory and later as well as over the last 100 years. If Conflict Archaeology writ large – that is to say, as a united field covering all periods of human conflict – is to have a distinctive contribution, then it is perhaps in its ability to draw on the strengths of archaeology more generally to achieve a broader and deeper appreciation of the human capacity for violence.

The structuring principle of this book has been that the three periods represented by Conflict Archaeology each exhibit particular agendas based on the concerns of a 'foundation' discipline external to archaeology:

- for prehistoric conflict, anthropology;
- for historic battlefields, military history;
- for modern Conflict Archaeology, heritage concerns.

However, these disciplinary agendas need not be restricted to the periods of study where they are most evident.

Anthropology

Out of the wider field of Historical Archaeology – especially as it has developed in North America – have emerged approaches to study the lifeways of people of the relatively recent past precisely through an anthropological perspective (Hicks and Beaudry 2006; and for its application in Britain, see Tarlow and West 1999). Conflict Archaeology, as it has developed so far, has the capacity to join in this wider endeavour and to study not just the practice of warfare but also its wider social context, its consequences and products and its ritual and symbolic aspects. Drawing upon anthropological inspiration rather than a rather narrow conception of military history, much more interesting questions should be amenable to archaeological investigation if we approach them adequately. In this respect, American historical archaeology has always considered itself an anthropological discipline, based on the understanding that archaeology is one of the areas of a four-field anthropology which also includes biological and cultural anthropology and linguistics. Accordingly, the work of American battlefield archaeologists is perceived by them as anthropologically informed, and this is highly evident in the work at Little Bighorn (Scott et al. 1989) where the contribution of anthropology is explicitly acknowledged. The role of biological anthropology in the study of human remains – stature, age and health profiles and trauma – is evident both at Little Bighorn, at Towton (Fiorato et al. 2000) and elsewhere. What is less evident outside of prehistoric study is any interest in the insights of social or cultural anthropology for the study of conflict.

As noted in Chapters 1 and 4, students of modern conflict often have a background in prehistory, and this in turn implies a knowledge of the application of anthropological theory. Issues of the use of material culture – the layout of buildings, access to material resources and evidence of the subversion of such mechanisms – raise issues concerning social control and power structures. Issues of civilian-military relations arise in a range of contexts. The disruption to ways of life caused by the construction of fortifications and military establishments, or of the encroachment of aggressive neighbours are also subject to investigation. The impact of Europeans on Indigenous conflict, especially by the provision of firearms, is evident in studies of Iroquois activity (Otterbein 1979) among others (see, e.g. Ferguson and Whitehead 1992). The damage to, or dislocation of, Indigenous populations as documented by Mallios (2006) and by Shapiro (1997, 7–13) in the case of Europeans in North America, and by the Inka Empire (D'Altroy 2005) in South America, also falls within a broadly interpreted Conflict Archaeology. Such examples may perhaps provide inspiration for the sorts of questions to be raised in relation to the effect of militarization in prehistoric, historic and modern contexts. These concerns are particularly evident in work examining the Greenham Common and Nevada Peace Camps (Schofield and Anderton 2000) where the confrontation between military and anti-military ideologies came into direct opposition. They are also highly evident in Anderton's (2002) examination of space and movement on military establishments. Anthropological concerns are less obvious but nonetheless present in attempts to understand military organizations as social institutions, as in the Roman army as a community (Goldsworthy and Adams 1999), and work on US Civil War military establishments (Balicki 2000). Issues of control – and attempts to subvert them – are of obvious interest not only in research at prisoner of war and other internment and concentration camps, but also arise in relation to the manner in which military activity impacts on civilian activity: the work on Irish cottier settlements is of direct relevance here (Frazer 2007), as are those on US Civil War rural and urban contexts (e.g. in Geier and Potter 2000), raising as they do echoes of Wileman's (2009) work on changes to landscape and environment in the context of prehistoric conflict.

The explicit introduction of anthropological issues and approaches into the interpretation of conflict of all periods may serve to give Conflict Archaeology the specific and distinctive role it requires to make a meaningful contribution to the understanding of a particular aspect of human society. This is not an argument for subsuming Conflict Archaeology into an 'anthropology of conflict', and thereby limiting its scope, but rather taking advantage of a disciplinary connection that already exists and turning it to the advantage of all the branches of the field, however named and whatever the specific period or material focus.

Military and security studies

Treating different styles of inter-societal conflict as 'war' in a Western sense invites the application of models of understanding derived from the Western experience – especially of a 'Clausewitzian' approach to mass violence as a rational practice of 'politics by other means' (e.g. Carman and Harding 2006b, 5–6). Going further than this is to take modern military manuals as a model for understanding the warfare of other cultures (Bleed and Scott 2011): this involves distinguishing 'levels' of war identified by current military practice such as 'strategy', 'operations' and 'tactics' and applying them to particular actions of cultures in the past. While quite directly applicable to an appreciation of Western styles of warfare since the mid- to late-nineteenth century, the strength of such sources for earlier periods and other parts of the world is to highlight differences of historically recent Western practice from that of others. In doing so, it has some affinity with the aims of the Bloody Meadows Project (Carman and Carman 2006; Carman 2012), which also seeks to identify differences and similarities in warfare practice across territorial, chronological and cultural boundaries.

While in general military history (as outlined in Chapter 1) offers a particular understanding of conflict, and readings of past military practice as equivalent to modern ones, it also provides a potential counterpoint to the findings of Conflict Archaeology. These can operate in two ways. As a search for origins – somewhat akin to the theme evident in prehistoric study (see Chapter 2) – modern military perspectives can be used as a basis from which to identify the first emergence of particular practices in the past. These can include a search through time for the first use of organized forces; of the separation of different types of troops; of the emergence of a specific function of military command from that of leading troops into action; and of the emergence of particular technologies, such as firearms, as well as armour, built defences, specialized military forts and fortresses as opposed to defended settlements and so on. The second manner is to challenge the assumptions very often made about conflict in the past – that 'military thinking' in the past is similar to that in the present. Where research into past activity indicates differences from those expected for the present or for a rational approach to warmaking, this may indicate a fundamentally different understanding from that of the modern age. Such differences may emerge in terms of the disposition of forces, the use of terrain, the selection of ground on – or conditions in – which to fight, failure to fight at all despite significant advantage or a commitment to fighting despite apparent overwhelming disadvantage. Rather than interpreting such divergences from appropriate behaviour as dysfunctional, they may instead represent indications of very different attitudes to violence and conflict.

Modern warmaking is a function of the nation-state and the idea that 'war made the state and the state made war' is one with a long history in anthropological (and indeed other) thinking. There does seem to be a good cross-cultural connection that can be made between states and warmaking, but it is not a simple correlation: while states may well make wars (as they still do), it is not so evident that the state as an institution is anything like an inevitable outcome of previous states of conflict (Claessen 2006). Rather, the state is a relatively rare occurrence until quite recent times, and the nation-state as we know it is a purely European invention from (mostly) the nineteenth century (Hobsbawm 1990; Gellner 1997). What does seem to correlate quite well is the relationship between state formation and conflict in the region beyond its borders (Ferguson and Whitehead 1992). From this perspective, the state represents not the thing that must be secured, but rather the threat to the security of others. Conflict Archaeology may perhaps be able to contribute something to our understanding of the connection between the state and security by its examination of conflict in the more distant past where the state is a rare or non-existent phenomenon. The recent development of the idea of 'human security' in critical security studies (Krause and Williams 1997) also changes the object of security from the state to people. From this perspective, the state, its agents and their activities can be seen as potential threats – among others – to the lives and welfare of individual human beings, families and other human communities. Taking the wider perspective that is emerging in Conflict Archaeology – especially the study of civilian refuges (e.g. Dewerdt and Willman 2003) and civilian responses to threats (e.g. Frazer 2007) – gives Conflict Archaeology a contribution beyond the bounds of its usual concerns.

Heritage

The perceived need to identify and record the – frequently ephemeral – remains of twentieth-century conflict drove the emergence of modern Conflict Archaeology. Similar concerns contributed to the rise of historic battlefield archaeology with the English Heritage (1995) Register of Historic Battlefields and the emergence of the US National Park Service Battlefields Protection Program (www.nps.gov/history/hps/abpp/index.htm) and continue with the development of similar exercises in Britain and Ireland, an inventory of historic battlefields in Flanders and planned similar exercises across Europe (one promoted by the ESTOC group covering significant battlesites of the entire historic period, the other out of Portugal relating more specifically to battles of the 'Hundred Years War' between France and England). There is also an ongoing concern for the range of threats to such sites, including landuse change and development, cultivation altering soil chemistry, contamination and, in particular, uncontrolled metal detecting (Sutherland and Holst 2005, 14–15; Foard 2008, 220–43). Saunders (2001) similarly points up the activities – and dangers to those involved – of uncontrolled retrieval from World War I battlesites. Piekarz (2007) approaches battlefields not as sites of research – as most Conflict Archaeologists do – but explicitly from the perspective of their public interpretation. In doing so, he emphasizes the different social roles they perform – as sites of memorialization, as an educational resource especially for historical study, as a recreation space and the more ephemeral notion of 'cultural asset' related to ideas of national and regional identity. He also identifies the factors that influence a battlesite's potential interest – its firm location at a particular point, its temporal distance from the present, its scale and its cultural or historical significance. This list apparently confirms the kind of judgements generally made in selecting sites for specific protection, but it relegates them to the category of historical places rather than archaeological resources (Carman 2005).

Similar ideas extend to sites of conflict of any type or period. It is doubtful whether many inhabitants of northern France recall the period when the region was ruled by Spain and made it a corridor for armies engaged in the almost permanent conflicts of the seventeenth century: any consciousness of war in the area will be dominated by memories of the two World Wars. Accordingly, it is unlikely that either battlefields or non-battlefield sites of the region associated with earlier conflict – such as fortified churches or houses, or underground refuges – will carry any particular interest unless they too are related to events of the last century. Prehistoric sites of violence may evoke even less public interest – the people are distant, their claim on the affection of the modern population may be overlain by myths of later immigration and population replacement and the sites themselves obscure and difficult to identify. Yet these places and structures are as integral a part of the story of human conflict in that region as any other and worthy of the same treatment: the same issues of identification, inventory and conservation therefore apply to all sites of conflict as apply to those of the modern world. In applying the same practices, connections between the more distant and more recent past become evident in terms of what these places may mean. Human beings have been very good at slaughtering each other for several millennia if the archaeological record speaks true (see e.g. Carman and Harding 2006a; Otto et al. 2006a) and both victims and perpetrators of that violence can be considered the ancestors of the current population. A Conflict Archaeology that seeks out, records and cares for all evidence of violence and conflict from all periods of history can develop a public perception of such behaviour over the long term of human history, offering a wider perspective. In particular, and for obvious reasons, it is more likely that modern populations are descended from the perpetrators of violence against others rather than the victims: making this clear may serve to mitigate the tendency to identify with the victim, and help the development of an 'archaeology of perpetrators' (Bernbeck and Pollock 2007) as a counterpoint.

Issues of identity

A recommendation (Pollard and Banks 2007, xiv) for a focus for First World War research on issues of cultural identity, 'its differences and similarities as reflected in soldiers', and indeed civilians', reactions to the environment of total war' reflects a similar agenda proposed for the ESTOC group who focus on pre-twentieth-century war in Europe (Carman 2012). In this view, Conflict Archaeology needs go beyond its current limitations to find a wider purpose for the study of those places which are indicative of past inter-group hostility. At present, such studies focus on the study of war – and sometimes other conflicts – as events in the past. However, they have much more to teach us than just that people can be violent towards one another: instead, it is possible to emphasize the complex social relationships that lie behind warfare and its practice. Conflict Archaeology can be a more 'bottom-up' way of studying the past than is conventional among other students of conflict, who are often more interested in leaders than in followers, and far less in the consequences of conflict than its causes. In looking to see how past conflict has created identities – rather than disrupting them – it becomes possible to make useful statements about what it is, and has been, to be 'European', 'American', 'Australian' or whatever other identity category is relevant.

Such an approach specifically addresses the problems of Conflict Archaeology as it has developed over the past two decades. The interest is far less in the form of conflict than in what that has to tell us about how people understood their world and how phenomena like war fitted into that world view. The focus shifts away from sites of conventional historical significance to those that represent the more typical conflict sites of their time – which also means looking beyond the well-known sites to find those more typical sites. Since they are the ones most likely to have been forgotten by conventional historical approaches, there is a need to develop specific research methods. As an expressly internationalist endeavour, a nationalist focus is closed: instead, a recognition of the inherently international nature of conflict in the past is forced upon us.

Wars and other forms of conflict create, among other things, new social relationships. The formation of a shared sense of experience among those who fought or were otherwise directly caught up in the fighting – as participants or as willing or unwilling observers – is something that war (or any powerful experience) will always create. A shared past of shifting alliances and enmities is something that has contributed to the idea of Europe as a continent-wide unity: frequently – only too frequently given the number of civil wars the states of Europe have experienced over the centuries – divisions within the populations of states have derived from or contributed to much wider conflicts between states. In such a case, it is not Anglo-French or Franco-German rivalry that drives the process of war: it is differences within populations over religion or choice of sovereign that have forced the pace. Cross-border friendships can, in these circumstances, be of greater significance than cross-border enmities: examples include the French Wars of Religion (1560–98) and Fronde (1648–53) and the War of the Spanish Succession in Spain (1702–15). The Battle of Oudenaarde in Flanders, Belgium, exemplifies these considerations.

The Battle of Oudenaarde (Lachaert 2008) was fought in July 1708 as part of the War of the Spanish Succession. It lasted less than a day and involved two polyglot armies: an allied coalition army of British, expatriate French, Irish, Dutch, Danish, Hanoverian, Hessian and Prussian troops, part of which was led by a Prince of the (Austrian) Empire, against a French army also containing 'Spanish' (probably southern Netherland – what we would call 'Belgian'), Irish, Bavarian, Swiss and possibly Italian contingents. The battle was fought in the sixth year of the war of which it was part, and it was the third battle where such forces had met; there had also been other operations in which they had all been involved, such as sieges and marches. We can expect that the experienced soldiers on both sides knew what was expected of them and what to expect, as would those attached to them. This too would be common on both sides. The experience of marching, of camps and of combat would be similar whether from France or Britain or elsewhere. Those attached to the armies – the 'camp followers' who provided so much in the way of welfare and medical aid, not to mention replacements for those lost from the firing line – would also have shared experience and comprehension of their involvement. The landscape of conflict was also something well known to the soldiers and followers of both armies: the main theatre of the war had been its seat since the opening campaign, and for some it would also have been the space of experience in previous wars. It was also the homeland of a few of the combatants. For the civilian inhabitants, the experience of living there would inevitably be altered by the presence of the armies. In 1708, Oudenaarde was a town with less than 20,000 inhabitants: the armies that fought – one of which marched through the town to the battle – each numbered some 80,000 soldiers. The impact upon the region of the descent of such large numbers would have been highly noticeable, even for the short space of time it took for them to pass through.

We can assume that the soldiers in both armies knew who their friends and allies were, and who the enemy was. These knowledges and understandings had been forged over a series of years involving shared hardship and mutual support with allies, and in a climate of hostility towards the common enemy. They would also have been created over a longer period: Franco-German hostility was a phenomenon that had its roots in the Middle Ages and would persist into the twentieth century; Anglo-French hostility was rather newer but again had deeper roots than more recent events; and Franco-Spanish, Anglo-Dutch and Dutch-Spanish hostility were factors that some in the military of both countries would remember from a few years previously and would serve to temper any ties of alliance. These types of knowledges and understandings would be common to the soldiers on both sides: the difference would lie in an appreciation of who was a friend and who an enemy. These structures of enmity and friendship would be part of the experience of soldiering and in turn would inform future constructions of such frameworks. The same is true of civilian onlookers: whereas the people of Ghent and

Brugge had abandoned the allies in favour of Spanish rule, the people of Oudenaarde had held to the allied cause. Old rivalries between the cities of Flanders would have informed and inflamed such decisions: so would newer bonds of loyalty and friendship. These kinds of relationships and reactions to an environment of war are perhaps universal, and widen the scope of Conflict Archaeology to an examination of the human dimensions of conflict.

Conclusion

Although frequently identified in terms of its parts – prehistoric, historic and modern, 'battlefield', 'Holocaust, internment' or 'occupation' archaeologies – Conflict Archaeology has the capacity to be greater than the sum of these parts. Its remit extends beyond particular periods or objects of study to all aspects of human violence and conflict. It can draw upon the range of influences from which the parts derive their inspiration – anthropology, military studies, heritage – to promote a wider, long-term understanding of how conflict contributes to the structure and development of society and culture, and how humans respond to situations of threat and danger. This makes Conflict Archaeology at once more interesting and more useful than a mere recording of violent incidents in the past: by combining an interest in different periods and the set of different approaches available to us, we may be able to provide a wider and deeper perspective on the human capacity for violence than any other field of enquiry. It has taken a while, but the possibility now emerges of achieving an aim from some years ago: that of 'the development of a 'voice' for archaeology in [one of] the important debates of our time' (Carman 1997a, 220).

Conclusion: Countering a critique of Conflict Archaeology

Chapter 1 of this book concluded with a section headed 'Critiquing Conflict Archaeology'. This section summarizes a response to this critique that derives from the argument developed over Chapters 2 to 5, drawing upon the positive aspects identified throughout and the common themes that emerge.

If particular ideas dominate, they are those of the breadth of scope and time-depth offered by a unified Conflict Archaeology. These are not exclusive to the study of conflict through its material legacy: they can be held to be the major strengths of archaeology as a discipline, since it examines human existence from the earliest humans to today and all aspects of human life. However, unlike other fields devoted to the study of conflict, archaeologists are neither bound by temporal limitations, geographical scope nor by a focus on particular material. Archaeologists can choose to examine any class of material anywhere and from any period of the human past and present. Doing so opens up the possibility of comparison and the search for cross-cultural similarities and differences that may inform study elsewhere. A further overarching issue is that of ethics. While issues of ethics are most evident in dealing with modern conflict – especially where human remains are involved – similar concerns can be extended to any era of the past. If there are certain aspects of human conflict we should be careful of in terms of investigation because of the types of violence they represent – the Holocaust is a prime example (Gilead et al. 2009; Sturdy Colls 2011) – that need for care also extends to any other example of similar activity, such as perhaps the Crow Creek massacre (Zimmerman 1997).

Other themes are also evident. The search for the origins of particular practices – for war and indeed violence itself; or particular kinds of warlike practice and attendant forms of social organization, such as specialized military castes – is one that derives from prehistoric approaches, but as suggested in Chapter 5 can be extended forward in time to other aspects of the field. At the same time, we can seek to identify not only similarities of practice in the past – as an 'origins'-based agenda would – but also those key differences in practice and form that indicate the range of possibilities in human organization and activity. These can include contributing to important current debates about the nature of conflict and the forms available, such as the debate concerning 'new' and 'global' wars (Reyna 2009). The social relations that underpin, are created and disrupted by conflict are also the subject of critical security studies (Krause and Williams 1997) but are limited to the contemporary world. The essential contribution that Conflict Archaeology can make is that of the long term and broad comparative perspective available to it.

A crucial need is for proponents and practitioners of the various strands of Conflict Archaeology to recognize and take advantage of the connections and synergies that bind us. To some extent this is already taking place, as the individual conference series that have been established over the past ten years or so share contributors, and as they expand their remit to include other aspects. The scope for work on prehistoric sites to inform that on historic or modern material, or for studies of more recent periods to throw light on earlier eras, is therefore growing. We share a common interest in how humans engage in and with hostility, aggression and violence; how different cultures incorporate or separate conflict from other aspects of life; how they organize for offence or defence; the conditions that create or prevent violence and war; the practices of conflict in different times and places and how they compare and contrast; and in the meanings and significance these carry for people in the past and present. Ultimately, we are all – whatever our specific focus of attention – in the business of memorialization. Whether prehistorian, historical archaeologist or student of contemporary material culture, we are united in a common concern for conflict in the past. We have much to learn from each other. That, put simply, is the message of this book.

Bibliography

Adam, F. 1991. *La sépulture collective de Saint-Remy-la-Calonne*. Quart-en-Réserve (Meuse). DRAC Imraine: Service regional de l'Archéologie.

Allen, M. W. 2006. 'Transformations in Maori warfare: toa, pa, and pu'. In E. N. Arkush and M. W. Allen (eds), *The Archaeology of Warfare: Prehistories of Raiding and Conquest*. Gainesville, FL: University of Florida Press, 184–213.

Allsop, D. and Foard, G. 2007. 'Case shot: an interim report on experimental firing and analysis to interpret early modern battlefield assemblages'. *Journal of Conflict Archaeology* 3(1), 111–46.

Anderton, M. J. 2002. 'Social space and social control: analysing movement and management on modern military sites'. In J. Schofield, W. G. Johnson and C. M. Beck (eds), *Matériel Culture: The Archaeology of Twentieth Century Conflict*. One World Archaeology 44. London: Routledge, 189–98.

Arkush, E. N. and Allen, M. W. 2006a. 'Introduction: archaeology and the study of war'. In E. N. Arkush and M. W. Allen (eds), *The Archaeology of Warfare: Prehistories of Raiding and Conquest*. Gainesville, FL: University of Florida Press, 1–19.

— (eds). 2006b. *The Archaeology of Warfare: Prehistories of Raiding and Conquest*. Gainesville, FL: University of Florida Press.

Atkinson, J. A., Banks, I. and O'Sullivan, B. (eds). 1996. *Nationalism and Archaeology: Scottish Archaeological Forum*. Glasgow: Cruithne Press.

Bailey, G. 1983. 'Concepts of time in quaternary prehistory'. *Annual Review of Anthropology* 12, 165–92.

Balicki, J. 2000. 'Defending the capital: the Civil War garrison at Fort C. F. Smith'. In C. R. Geier and S. R. Potter (eds), *Archaeological Perspectives on the American Civil War*. Gainesville, FL: University Press of Florida, 125–47.

—. 2007. 'The Confederate cantonment at Evansport, Virginia'. In D. Scott, L. Babits and C. Haecker (eds), *Fields of Conflict: Battlefield Archaeology from the Roman Empire to the Korean War. Volume 2: Nineteenth and Twentieth Century Fields of Conflict*. Westport, CT: Praeger, 255–77.

Banks, I. 2007. 'Ghosts in the desert: the archaeological investigation of a sub-Saharan battlefield'. *Journal of Conflict Archaeology* 3(1), 1–28.

Beck, C. M. 2002. 'The archaeology of scientific experiments at a nuclear testing ground'. In J. Schofield, W. G. Johnson and C. M. Beck (eds), *Matériel Culture: The Archaeology of Twentieth Century Conflict*. One World Archaeology 44. London: Routledge, 65–79.

Becker, A. 2004. 'Art, material life and disaster: civilian and military prisoners of war'. In N. Saunders (ed.), *Matters of Conflict: Material Culture, Memory and the First World War*. London: Routledge, 26–34.

Bennike, P. and Brade, A. -E. 1999. *Middelalderens sygdomme og behandlingformer in Danmark*. Københavns Universitet: Medicinsk-Historisk Museum.

Bernbeck, R. and Pollock, S. 2007. '"Grabe, Wo Du Sehst!" An archaeology of perpetrators'. In Y. Hamilakis and P. Duke (eds), *Archaeology and Capitalism: From Ethics to Politics*. One World Archaeology 54. Walnut Creek, CA: West Coast Press, 217–34.

Black, J. 2004. 'Thanks for the memory: war memorials, spectatorship and the trajectories of commemoration'. In N. Saunders (ed.), *Matters of Conflict: Material Culture, Memory and the First World War*. London: Routledge, 134–48.

Bleed, P. and Scott, D. 2011. 'Contexts for conflict: conceptual tools for interpreting archaeological reflections on warfare'. *Journal of Conflict Archaeology* 6(1), 42–64.

Brady, C., Byrnes, E., Cooney, G. and O'Sullivan, A. 2007. An archaeological study of the Battle of the Boyne at Oldbridge, Co. Meath. *Joyurnal of Conflict Archaeology* 3(1), 53–77.

Bradley, R. Forthcoming. 'Lost in time: new perspectives on locating mass graves on English Civil War battlefields'. In J. Carman, P. Garwood, S. Morewood and S. Shepherd (eds), *Conflict, Violence and Landscapes of Death. IAA Interdisciplinary Series Vol. 3: Studies in Archaeology, History, Literature and Art*. BAR International Series. Oxford, Archaeopress.

Bridgford, S. 1997. 'Mightier than the pen? An edgewise look at Bronze Age swords'. In J. Carman (ed.), *Material Harm: Archaeological Studies of War and Conflict*. Glasgow: Cruithne Press, 95–115.

Brooke, R. 1854. *Visits to the Fields of Battle in England of the Fifteenth Century*. London, John Russell Smith reprinted 1975, Dursley, Alan Sutton.

Brown, M. 2011. 'Whose heritage? Archaeology, heritage and the military'. In P. G. Stone (ed.), *Cultural Heritage, Ethics and the Military*. Heritage Matters. Woodbridge: The Boydell Press, 129–38.

Bruce, D. and Creighton, O. 2006. 'Contested identities: the doissonant heritage of European town walls and walled towns'. *International Journal of Heritage Studies* 12(3), 234–54.

Buchli, V. and Lucas, G. 2001. *Archaeologies of the Contemporary Past*. London: Routledge.

Bulgrin, L. E. 2006. 'The Tudela Site: fire and steel over Saipan, 15 June 1944'. In T. Pollard and I. Banks (eds), *Past Tense: Studies in the Archaeology of Conflict*. Leiden: Brill = *Journal of Conflict Archaeology* 1, 1–18.

Burström. M., Acosta, T. D., Noriega, E. G., Gustafsson, A., Hernández, I., Karlsson, H., Jaramillo, J. M. P., Jaramillo, J. R. R. and Westergaard, B. 2009. 'Memories of a world crisis: the archaeology of a former Soviet nuclear missile site in Cuba'. *Journal of Social Archaeology*, 9(3), 296–318.

Burström. M., Gustafsson, A. and Karlsson, H. 2011. World Crisis in Ruin: the archaeology of the former Sovirt nuclear missile sites in Cuba. Lindome: Bricoleur Pres.

Burt, R., Bradford, J., Dickson, B., Everett, M. E., Warden, R. and Woodcock, D. 2007. 'Pointe-du-Hoc battlefield, Normandy, France'. In D. Scott, L. Babits and C. Haecker (eds), *Fields of Conflict: Battlefield Archaeology from the Roman Empire to the Korean War. Volume 2:*

Nineteenth and Twentieth Century Fields of Conflict. Westport, CT: Praeger, 383–97.

Carman, J. 1997a. 'Introduction; approaches to violence'. In J. Carman (ed.), *Material Harm: Archaeological Studies of War and Conflict.* Glasgow: Cruithne Press, 1–23.

— (ed.). 1997b. *Material Harm: Archaeological Studies of War and Conflict.* Glasgow: Cruithne Press.

—. 2002a. *Archaeology and Heritage: An Introduction.* London and New York: Continuum.

—. 2002b. 'Paradox in places: 20th century battlefields in long-term perspective'. In J. Schofield, W. G. Johnson and C. Beck (eds), *Matériel Culture: The Archaeology of 20th Century Conflict.* London: Routledge, 9–21.

—. 2005. Battlefields as cultural resources. *Post-Medieval Archaeology* 392, 215–23.

—. 2012. 'Past war and European identity: making Conflict Archaeology useful'. In S. Ralph (ed.), *The Archaeology of Violence: Interdisciplinary Approaches.* Albany: State University of New York Press, 258–77.

Carman, J. and Carman, P. 2006. *Bloody Meadows: Investigating Landscapes of Battle.* Stroud: Sutton.

—. 2007. 'From rhetoric to research: the Bloody Meadows project as a pacifist response to war'. In L. McAtackney, M. Palus and A. Piccini (eds), *Contemporary and Historical Archaeology in Theory. Papers from the 2003 and 2004 CHAT Conferences.* BAR International Series 1677. Oxford: Archaeopress, 109–14.

Carman, J. and Harding, A. 2006a. 'Introduction'. In J. Carman and A. Harding (eds), *Ancient Warfare: Archaeological Perspectives.* Stroud: Sutton, 1–9.

— (eds). 2006b. *Ancient Warfare: Archaeological Perspectives.* Stroud: Sutton.

Carr, G. 2010. 'The archaeology of occupation, 1940–2009: a case study from the Channel Islands'. *Antiquity* 84, 161–74.

—. 2011. 'Beyond Normandy in World War Two: occupation, resistance and remembrance'. *Journal of Conflict Archaeology* 6(2), 173–76.

Casella, E. C. 2007. *The Archaeology of Institutional Confinement*. The American Experience in Archaeological Perspective. Gainesville, FL: University of Florida Press.

Chapman, J. 2006. 'The origins of warfare in the prehistory of Central and Eastern Europe'. In J. Carman and A. Harding (eds), *Ancient Warfare: Archaeological Perspectives*. Stroud: Sutton, 101–42.

Christiansen, H. 2002. 'Forgotten and refound military structures in the central Pacific: examples from the Marshall Islands'. In J. Schofield, W. G. Johnson and C. M. Beck (eds), *Matériel Culture: The Archaeology of Twentieth Century Conflict*. One World Archaeology 44. London: Routledge, 58–64.

Claessen, H. 2006. 'War and state formation: what's the connection'? In T. Otto, H. Thrane and H. Vandkilde (eds) 2006, *Warfare and Society: Archaeological and Social Anthropological Perspectives*. Aarhus: Aarhus Universitetsforlag, 217–26.

Clark, K. 2002. 'In small things remembered: significance and vulnerability in the management of Robben Island World Heritage Site'. In J. Schofield, W. G. Johnson and C. M. Beck (eds), *Matériel Culture: The Archaeology of Twentieth Century Conflict*. One World Archaeology 44. London: Routledge, 266–80.

Cloutier, P. and L'Anglais, P. -L. 2009. 'The Saint-Louis forts and chateaux site: archaeology in the heart of New France'. *Post-Medieval Archaeology* 43(1), 106–24.

Coad, J. 2005. 'Warfare and defence: what next'? *Post-Medieval Archaeology* 39(2), 224–32.

Cobo, E. P., Vázquez, J. S., Moralers, J. R., López, J. M., Martínez-Granero, A. B. and García, M. A. 2008. 'Arqueología de la batalla de Jarama'. *Complutum* 19(2), 63–87.

Connell, S. V. and Silverstein, J. E. 2006. 'From Laos to Mesoamerica: battlegrounds between superpowers'. In E. N. Arkush and M. W. Allen (eds, *The Archaeology of Warfare: Prehistories of Raiding and Conquest*. Gainesville, FL: University of Florida Press, 394–433.

Corsane, G. 2006. 'Robben Island: facing the challenges of creating a National Museum in a World Heritage Site'. In J. Schofield, A. Klausmeier and L. Purbroick (eds), *Remapping the Field: New Approaches in Conflict Archaeology.* Berlin: Westkreuz-Verlag, 64–71.

Courtney, P. 2001. 'The archaeology of the early-modern siege'. In T. Freeman and A. Pollard (eds), *Fields of Conflict: progress and prospects in battlefield archaeology, proceedings of a conference held in the Department of Archaeology, University of Glasgow,* April 2000. BAR International Series 958. Oxford: Archaeopress, 105–15.

Crossland, Z. 2002. 'Violent spaces: conflict over the reappearance of Argentina's disappeared'. In J. Schofield, W. G. Johnson and C. M. Beck, C. M. (eds), *Matériel Culture: The Archaeology of Twentieth Century Conflict.* One World Archaeology 44. London: Routledge, 115–31.

Cunha, E. and Silva, A. M. 1997. 'War lesions from the famous Portuguese medieval battle of Aljubarotta'. *International Journal of Oseteoarchaeology* 7, 595–99.

Curtis, J. 2009. 'Relations between archaeologists and the military in the case of Iraq'. *Papers from the Institute of Archaeology* 19, 2–8.

D'Altroy, T. N. 2005. 'Remaking the social landscape: colonization in the Inka empire'. In G. J. Stein, *The Archaeology of Colonial Encounters.* School of American Research Advanced Seminar Series. Santa Fe: School of American Research Press, 263–96.

Demuth, V. 2009 '"Those who survived the battlefields": archaeological investigations at a prisoner of war camp near Quedlinburg (Harz/Germany) from the First World War'. *Journal of Conflict Archaeology* 5(1), 163–82.

Dewerdt, H. and Willman, F. 2003. 'Concepteurs et Conception des muches du nord de la France'. In H. C. Derwedt (ed.), *Concepteurs at Conception d'Espaces Souterrains: actes du colloque international de subterranologie, Auxi-le-Chateau, 8–10 May 1999.* Bulletin Spécial du Cercle Histoirique d'Auxi-le-Chateau 2.

Dewilde, M., Pype, P., de Meyer, M., Demeyere, F., Lammens, W., Degryse, J., Wyffels, F. and Saunders, N. 2004. Belgium's new department of First

World War archaeology. *Antiquity* 78. www.antiquity.ac.uk/projgall/saunders/index.html. Accessed 16 March 2012.

Diaz-Andreu, M. and Champion, T. (eds). 1996. *Nationalism and Archaeology in Europe*. London: Routledge.

Dolff-Bonekämper, G. 2002. 'The Berlin Wall: an archaeological site in progress'. In J. Schofield, W. G. Johnson and C. M. Beck (eds), *Matériel Culture: The Archaeology of Twentieth Century Conflict*. One World Archaeology 44. London: Routledge, 236–48.

Doran, L. 2007. Defending the sacred: from Crac de Chevalier to Aghavillier – a common thread. *History Ireland* 15(6), 15–19.

Doyle, P. and Bennett, M. R. (eds). 2002. *Fields of Battle: Terrain in Military History*. Dordrecht: Kluwer.

Doyle, P., Babits, L. and Pringle, J. 2007. '"For you the war is over": finding the Great Escape tunnel at Stalag Luft III'. In D. Scott, L. Babits and C. Haecker (eds), *Fields of Conflict: Battlefield Archaeology from the Roman Empire to the Korean War. Volume 2: Nineteenth and Twentieth Century Fields of Conflict*. Westport, CT: Praeger, 398–416.

Doyle, P. Barton, P., Rosenbaum, M. S., Vandewall, J. and Jacobs, K. 2002a. 'Geo-environmental implications of military mining in Flanders, Belgium, 1914–1918'. *Environmental Geology* 43, 57–71.

Doyle, P., Bennett, M. R., Macleod, R. and Mackay, L. 2002b. 'Terrain and the Messines Ridge, Belgium, 1914–1918'. In P. Doyle and M. R. Bennett (eds), *Fields of Battle: Terrain in Military History*. Dordrecht: Kluwer, 205–224.

English Heritage. 1995. *Register of Historic Battlefields*. London, English Heritage.

Ewart, G. and Gallagher, D. 2010. 'The fortifications of Fort George, Ardersier, near Inverness: archaeological investigations 1990–2005'. *Post-Medieval Archaeology* 44(1), 105–34.

Farrell, M. and Burton, J. 2011. 'Gordon Hirabayashi, the Tucsonians and the U.S. constitution: negotiating reconciliation in a land of exile'. In A. Myers and G. Moshenska (eds), *Archaeologies of Internment*. New York: Springer, 89–110.

Faulkner, N., Saunders, N. and Winterburn, J. 2007. *The Great Arab Revolt Project. 2006 and 2007 Field Seasons.* GARP.www.jordan1914-18archaeology.org/report2.htm. Accessed 17 March 2012.

Ferguson, R. B. 2006. 'Archaeology, cultural anthropology and the origin and intensification of war'. In E. N. Arkush and M. W. Allen (eds), *The Archaeology of Warfare: Prehistories of Raiding and Conquest.* Gainesville, FL: University of Florida Press, 469–523.

Ferguson, R. B. (ed.). 1984. *Warfare, Culture and Environment: Studies in Anthropology.* Orlando, FL: Academic Press.

Ferguson, R. B. and Whitehead, N. L. (eds). 1992. *War in the Tribal Zone: Expanding States and Indigenous Warfare.* Santa Fe NM: School of American Research Press.

Ferris, I. 2006. 'Suffering in silence: the political aesthetics of pain in Antonoine art'. In T. Pollard and I. Banks (eds) *Past Tense: Studies in the Archaeology of Conflict.* Leiden: Brill = *Journal of Conflict Archaeology* 1, 67–92.

Fiorato, V., Boylston, A. and Knusel, C. 2000. *Blood Red Roses: The Archaeology of a Mass Grave from the Battle of Towton AD 1461.* Oxford: Oxbow.

Fiset, R. and Samson, G. 2009. 'Charlesbourg-Royal and France-Roy (1541–43): France's first colonization attempt in the Americas'. *Post-Medieval Archaeology* 43(1), 48–70.

Foard, G. 1995. *Naseby. The Decisive Campaign.* Whitstable: Pryor Publications.

—. 2001. 'The archaeology of attack: battles and sieges of the English Civil War'. In T. Freeman and A. Pollard (eds), *Fields of Conflict: progress and prospects in battlefield archaeology, proceedings of a conference held in the Department of Archaeology, University of Glasgow,* April 2000, Oxford, BAR International Series 958, Archaeopress, 87–104.

—. 2003. 'Sedgemoor 1685: historic terrain, the "archaeology of battles" and the revision of military history'. *Landscapes* 4(2), 5–15.

—. 2005. *History from the Field: The Edgehill Battlefield Survey.* London, Battlefields Trust.

—. 2006. 'Review of *Bloody Meadows* by Carman and Carman'. *Post-Medieval Archaeology* 402, 424–25.

—. 2007. 'English battlefields 991–1685: a review of problems and potentials'. In D. Scott, L. Babits and C. Haecker (eds), *Fields of Conflict: Battlefield Archaeology from the Roman Empire to the Korean War. Volume 1: Searching for War in the Ancient and Early Modern World.* Westport, CT: Praeger, 133–59.

—. 2008. *Conflict in the pre-industrial landscape of England: a resource assessment.* Leeds: University of Leeds. Available at: http://battlefieldstrust.com/resource-centre/battlefieldsuk/periodpageview.asp?pageid=831. Accessed 17 August 2011.

Foot, W. 2004. Defence Areas: a national study of Second World War anti-invasion landscapes in England. London: English Heritage.

Fraser, A. H., and Brown, M. 2007. 'Mud, blood and missing men: excavations at Serre, Somme, France'. *Journal of Conflict Archaeology* 3(1), 147–71.

Frazer, W. O. 2007. 'Field of fire: evidence for wartime conflict in a 17th century cottier settlement in County Meath, Ireland'. *Journal of Conflict Archaeology* 3(1), 173–95.

Freeman, T. and Pollard, A. (eds). 2001. *Fields of Conflict: Progress and Prospects in Battlefield Archaeology, Proceedings of a Conference Held in the Department of Archaeology, University of Glasgow, April 2000.* BAR International Series 958. Oxford: Archaeopress.

Fried, M., Harris, M. and Murphy, R. (eds). 1968. *War: The Anthropology of Armed Conflict and Aggression.* New York: Natural History Press.

Gaffney, V., Haldon, J. and Theodoropoulos, G. Forthcoming. *Manzikert: Medieval Warfare on the GRID.*

Geier, C. R. and Potter, S. R. (eds). 2000. *Archaeological Perspectives on the American Civil War.*Gainesville, FL: University Press of Florida.

Gellner, E. 1997. *Nationalism.* London: Weidenfeld and Nicolson.

Gilead, I., Haimi, Y. and Mazurek, W. 2009. 'Excavating Nazi extermination centres'. *Present Pasts* 1, 10–39.

Gleeson, F. 2011. *Women and children in prehistoric violence.* Unpublished MPhil dissertation, University of Birmingham, December 2011.

Gojak, D. 2002. '"So suspicious of enemies": Australia's late nineteenth- and twentieth-century coastal defences, their archaeology and interpretation'. In J. Schofield, W. G. Johnson and C. M. Beck (eds), *Matériel Culture: The Archaeology of Twentieth Century Conflict*. One World Archaeology 44. London: Routledge, 159–71.

Goldsworthy, A., and Adams, C. 1999. 'The Roman army as a community: including papers of a conference held at Birkbeck College, University of London, on 11–12 January 1997'. *Journal of Roman Archaeology Supplementary Series No. 34*.

González-Ruibal, A. 2007. 'Making things public: archaeologies of the Spanish Civil War'. *Public Archaeology* 6(4), 203–26.

—. 2011a. 'The archaeology of internment in Francoist Spain (1936–1952)'. In A. Myers and G. Moshenska (eds), *Archaeologies of Internment*. New York: Springer, 53–74.

—. 2011b. 'Digging Franco's trenches: an archaeological investigation of a Nationalist position from the Spanish Civil War'. *Journal of Conflict Archaeology* 6(2), 97–123.

Graves Brown, P. (ed.). 2000. *Matter, Materiality and Modern Culture*. London: Routledge

Greene, J. A. and Scott, D. D. 2004. *Finding Sand Creek: history, archaeology and the 1864 massacre site*. Norman O: University of Oklahoma Press.

Grguric, N. K. 2008. 'Fortified homesteads: the architecture of fear in frontier South Australia and the Northern Territory, ca. 1847–1885'. *Journal of Conflict Archaeology* 4(1/2), 59–86.

Guilane, J. and Zammit, J. 2005. *The Origins of War: violence in prehistory*. Translated by M. Hersey. Oxford: Blackwell.

Guimont, J. 2009. Fort Saint-Louis and other 17th-century fortification works discovered recently in Québec City. *Post-Medieval Archaeology* 43(1) 140–55.

Haas, J. (ed.). 1990. *The Anthropology of War*. Cambridge: Cambridge University Press.

— 1999. 'The origins of war and ethnic violence'. In J. Carman and A. Harding (eds), *Ancient Warfare: Archaeological Perspectives*, Stroud, Sutton, 11–24.

Haecker, C. M. 2001. 'The official explanation versus the archaeological record of a US-Mexican War battle'. In T. Freeman and A. Pollard (eds), *Fields of Conflict: Progress and Prospects in Battlefield Archaeology, Proceedings of a Conference Held in the Department of Archaeology,* University of Glasgow, April 2000. BAR International Series 958. Oxford: Archaeopress, 135–42.

Haecker, C. M. and Mauck, J. G. 1997. *On the Prairie of Palo Alto: Historical Archaeology of the U.S.–Mexican War Battlefield.* College Station, TX: Texas A&M University Press.

Haecker, C. M., Oster, E. A., Enríquez, A. M. and Elliott, M. L. 2007. 'Indian resistance in New Spain: the 1541 battlefield of Peñol de Nochistlán, an exemplar of Indigenous resistance'. In D. Scott, L. Babits and C. Haecker (eds), *Fields of Conflict: Battlefield Archaeology from the Roman Empire to the Korean War* 2 vols. Westport, CT: Praeger, 174–92.

Haldon, J. F. 2006. 'Introduction: why study logistical systems'? In J. F. Haldon (ed.), *General Issues in the Study of Medieval Logistics.* History of Warfare 36. Leiden: Brill, 1–37.

Halsall, G. 1989. 'Anthropology and the study of pre-conquest warfare and society: the Ritual War in Anglo-Saxon England'. In S. C. Hawkes (ed.), *Weapons and Warfare in Anglo-Saxon England,* Oxford University Committee for Archaeology Monograph 21, Oxford, Oxbow Books, 155–77.

Hamilakis, Y. 2003. 'Iraq, stewardship and "the record": an ethical crisis for archaeology'. *Public Archaeology* 3(2), 104–11.

—. 2009. 'The "war on terror" and the military-archaeology complex: Iraq, ethics and neo-colonialism'. *Archaeologies* 5(1), 39–65.

Hanson, V. D. 1989. *The Western Way of War.* Infantry Battle in Classical Greece. Oxford: Oxford University Press.

Harding, A. 2007. *Warriors and Weapons in Bronze Age Europe.* Budapest: Archaeolongua.

Harrison, R. and Schofield, J. 2010. *After Modernity: Archaeological Approaches to the Contemporary Past.* Oxford: Oxford University Press.

Hicks, D. and Beaudry, M. C. 2006. 'Introduction: the place of historical archaeology'. In D. Hicks and M. C. Beaudry (eds), *The Cambridge Companion to Historical Archaeology.* Cambridge: Cambridge University Press, 1–9.

Hobsbawm, E. 1990. *Nations and Nationalism Since 1780: Programme, Myth, Reality.* Cambridge, Cambridge University Press.

Homann, A. and Weise, J. 2009. 'The archaeological investigation of two battles and an engagement in North Germany in the 19th century: as summary of work carried out at Idstedt, Grossbeeren and Lauenburg'. *Journal of Conflict Archaeology* 5(1), 27–56.

Hoshower-Leppo, L. 2002. 'Missing in action: searching for America's war dead'. In J. Schofield, W. G. Johnson and C. M. Beck (eds), *Matériel Culture: The Archaeology of Twentieth Century Conflict.* One World Archaeology 44. London: Routledge, 80–90.

Ingelmark, B. E. 1939. 'The skeletons'. In B. Thordemann (ed.), *Armour from the Battle of Wisby 1361.* Stockholm: Vitterhets Historie Och Anikvitets Acadamien, 149–210.

Jacobs, K. 2007. *Nieuwport Sector 1917.* Dorpstraat: de Krijger.

Jarman, N. 2002. 'Troubling remnants: dealing with the remains of conflict in Northern Ireland'. In J. Schofield, W. G. Johnson and C. M. Beck (eds), *Matériel Culture: The Archaeology of Twentieth Century Conflict.* One World Archaeology 44. London: Routledge, 281–95.

Jarvis, H. 2002. 'Mapping Cambodia's "killing fields"'. In J. Schofield, W. G. Johnson and C. M. Beck (eds), *Matériel Culture: The Archaeology of Twentieth Century Conflict.* One World Archaeology 44. London: Routledge, 91–102.

Johnson, D. M. 2007. 'Apache Victory Against the US Dragoons: the battle of Cieneguilla, New Mexico'. In D. Scott, L. Babits and C. Haecker (eds), *Fields of Conflict: Battlefield Archaeology from the Roman Empire to the Korean War* 2 vols. Westport, CT: Praeger, 235–54.

Johnson, M. 2002. Behind the Castle Gate: from Medieval to Renaissance. London: Routledge.

Johnson, W. G. 2002. 'Archaeological examination of Cold War architecture: a reactionary cultural response to the threat of nuclear war'. In J. Schofield, W. G. Johnson and C. M. Beck (eds), *Matériel Culture: The Archaeology of Twentieth Century Conflict*. One World Archaeology 44. London: Routledge, 227–35.

Jones, C. 2011. *Finding Fulford: The Search for the First Battle of 1066*. London, WPS.

Jørgensen, A. N. 1999. *Waffen und Gräber: typolische und chronologische Studien zu skandinavischen Waffengräbern 520/530 bis 900 nr. Chr*. Copenhagen: det Kongelige Nordiske Oldskriftselkab.

Kauppi, U.-R. 2002. 'The Salpa Line: a monument of the future and the traces of war in the Finnish cultural landscape'. In J. Schofield, W. G. Johnson and C. M. Beck (eds), *Matériel Culture: The Archaeology of Twentieth Century Conflict*. One World Archaeology 44. London: Routledge, 49–57.

Keeley, L. H. 1996. *War Before Civilization: The Myth of the Peaceful Savage*. Oxford and New York: Oxford University Press.

Keegan, J. 1993. *A History of Warfare*, London, Hutchinson.

Kidd, W. 2004. 'The lion, the angel and the war memorial: some French sites revisited'. In N. Saunders (ed.), *Matters of Conflict: Material Culture, Memory and the First World War*. London: Routledge, 149–65.

Klausmeier, A. and Schmidt, L. 2006. 'Commemorating the uncomfortable: the Berlin Wall'. In J. Schofield, A. Klausmeier and L. Purbroick (eds), *Remapping the Field: New Approaches in Conflict Archaeology*. Berlin: Westkreuz-Verlag, 22–7.

Knarrström, B. 2006. *Slagfältet: om bataljen vid Lanskrona 1677 och finden från den första arkeologiska undersökningen av ett svenskt slagfält*. Saltsjö-Duvnäs: Efron and Dotter.

Kohl, P. L. and Fawcett, C. (eds). 1995. *Nationalism, Politics and the Practice of Archaeology*. Cambridge: Cambridge University Press.

Kokkinidou, D. and Nikolaidou, M. 1997. 'Neolitic enclosures in Greek Macedonia: violent and non-violent aspects of territorial demarcation'.

In J. Carman and A. Harding (eds), *Ancient Warfare: Archaeological Perspectives*. Stroud: Sutton, 89–100.

Krause, K. and Williams, M. C. 1997. *Critical Security Studies: Concepts and Cases*. London: UCL Press.

Kristiansen, K. 1999. 'The emergence of warrior aristocracies in later European prehistory and their long-term history'. In J. Carman and A. Harding (eds), *Ancient Warfare: Archaeological Perspectives*. Stroud: Sutton, 175–90.

Kusimba, C. M. 2006. 'Slavery and warfare in African chiefdoms'. In E. N. Arkush and M. W. Allen (eds), *The Archaeology of Warfare: Prehistories of Raiding and Conquest*. Gainesville, FL: University of Florida Press, 214–49.

Lachaert, P.-J. (ed.). 2008. *Oudenaarde 1708: een stad, een konig, een veldheer*. Leuven/Oudenaarde: Stad Oudenaarde, Davidsfond.

Lake, J. 2002. 'Historic airfields: evaluation and conservation'. In J. Schofield, W. G. Johnson and C. M. Beck (eds), *Matériel Culture: The Archaeology of Twentieth Century Conflict*. One World Archaeology 44. London: Routledge, 172–88.

Lake, J., Monckton, L. and Morrison, K. 2006. 'Interpreting Bletchley Park'. In J. Schofield, A. A. Klausmeier and L. Purbroick (eds), *Remapping the Field: New Approaches in Conflict Archaeology*. Berlin: Westkreuz-Verlag, 49–57.

Laumbach, K. W. 2007. 'Buffalo Soldiers versus the Apache: the Battle in Hembrillo Basin'. In D. Scott, L. Babits and C. Haecker (eds), *Fields of Conflict: Battlefield Archaeology from the Roman Empire to the Korean War* 2 vols. Westport, CT: Praeger, 336–58.

Leech, R. 2002. 'The battlefield of the Dukla Pass: an archaeological perspective on the end of the Cold War in Europe'. In J. Schofield, W. G. Johnson and C. M. Beck (eds), *Matériel Culture: The Archaeology of Twentieth Century Conflict*. One World Archaeology 44. London: Routledge, 41–8.

Lenihan, P. 2007. 'Unhappy campers: Dundalk (1689) and after'. *Journal of Conflict Archaeology* 3(1), 197–216.

Levitch, M. 2004. 'The Great War remembered: the fragmentation of the world's largest painting'. In N. Saunders (ed.), *Matters of Conflict: Material Culture, Memory and the First World War*. London: Routledge, 90–108.

Lillington-Martin, C. 2007. 'Archaeological and ancient literary evidence for a battle near Dara Gap, Turkey, AD 530: topography, texts and trenches'. In A. S. Lewin, P. Pellegrini and Z. Fiema (eds), *The Late Roman Army in the Near East from Diocletian to the Arab Conquest Proceedings of a Colloquium Held at Potenza, Acerenza and Matera, Italy* (May 2005). BAR International Series S1717. Oxford: Archaeopress, 299–311.

Loechl, S. K., Enscore, S. I., Tooker, M. W. and Batzli, S. A. 2009. *Guidelines for Identifying and Evaluating Historic Military Landscapes*. Legacy Resource Management Programme Project 05-197, ERDC/CERL TR-09-6. Arlington: US Army Corps of Engineers, Engineer Research and Development Centre.

Malan, A. and Soudien, C. 2002. 'Managing heritage in District Six, Cape Town: conflicts past and present'. In J. Schofield, W. G. Johnson C. M. and Beck (eds), *Matériel Culture: The Archaeology of Twentieth Century Conflict*. One World Archaeology 44. London: Routledge, 249–65.

Mallios, S. 2006. *The Deadly Politics of Giving: Exchange and Violence at Ajacan, Roanoke and Jamestown*. Tuscaloosa: University of Alabama Press.

Mandzy, A. 2007. 'Tartars, Cossacks and the Polish Army: the battle of Zboriv'. In D. Scott, L. Babits and C. Haecker (eds), *Fields of Conflict: Battlefield Archaeology from the Roman Empire to the Korean War* 2 vols. Westport, CT: Praeger, 193–207.

Manning-Sterling, E. 2000. 'Antietam: the cultural impact of battle on an agrarian landscape'. In C. R. Geier and S. R. Potter (eds), *Archaeological Perspectives on the American Civil War*. Gainesville, FL: University Press of Florida, 188–216.

Martin, D. L. and Frayer, D. W. (eds). 1997. *Troubled Times: Violence and Warfare in the Past*. Amsterdam: Gordon and Breach.

Matoušek, V. 2006. 'Building a model of a field fortification of the "Thirty Years War" near Olbramov, Czech Republic'. In T. Pollard and I. Banks (eds), *Past Tense: Studies in the Archaeology of Conflict*. Leiden: Brill = *Journal of Conflict Archaeology* 1, 115–32.

McAtackney, L. 2007. 'The contemporary politics of landscape at the Long Kesh/Maze Proson site, Northern Ireland'. In D. Hicks, L. McAtackney, and G. Fairclough (eds), *Envisioning Landscape: Situations and Standpoints in Archaeology and Heritage*. One World Archaeology 52. Walnut Creek, CA: Left Coast Press, 30–54.

McBride, W. S., Andrews, S. C. and Coughlin, S. P. 2000. '"For the convenience and comforts of the soldiers and employees at the depot": archaeology of the Owens' House/Post Office complex, Camp Nelson, Kentucky'. In C. R. Geier and S. R. Potter (eds), *Archaeological Perspectives on the American Civil War*. Gainesville, FL: University Press of Florida, 99–124.

Meredith, J. with Anderson, S., Egan, G., Higgins, D. and Pattison, P. 2008. 'Excavation at Languard Fort: an investigation of the 17th-century defences'. *Post-Medieval Archaeology* 42(2), 229–75.

Messenger, P. M. and Smith, G. S. (eds). 2010. *Cultural Heritage Management: A Global Perspective*. Gainesville, FL: University Press of Florida.

de Meyer, M. and Pype, P. 2007. 'Scars of the Great War Western Flanders, Belgium'. In D. Scott, L. Babits and C. Haecker (eds), *Fields of Conflict: Battlefield Archaeology from the Roman Empire to the Korean War*, 2 vols. Westport, CT: Praeger, 259–82.

Millard, K., Burke, C., Stiff, D. and Redden, A. 2009. 'Detection of a low-relief 18th-century British siege trench using LiDAR vegetation penetration capabilities at Fort Beaséjour-Fort Cumberland National Historic Site, Canada'. *Geoarchaeology* 24(5), 576–88.

Molloy, B. (ed.). 2007. *The Cutting Edge: Archaeological Studies in Combat and Weaponry*. Stroud: The History Press.

Monckton, L. 2006. 'Bletchley Park, Buckinghamshire: the architecture of the Government Code and Cypher School'. *Post-Medieval Archaeology* 40(2), 291–300.

Moshenska, G. 2008. 'Ethics and ethical critique in the archaeology of modern conflict'. *Norwegian Archaeological Review* 41, 159–75.

—. 2009. 'Resonant materiality and violent remembering: archaeology, memory and bombing'. *International Journal of Heritage Studies* 15(1), 44–56.

Moshenska, G. and Myers, A. 2011. 'An introduction to archaeologies of internment'. In A. Myers and G. Moshenska (eds), *Archaeologies of Internment*. New York: Springer, 1–21.

Moussette, M. 2009. 'A universe under strain: Amerindian nations in north-eastern North America in the 16th century'. *Post-Medieval Archaeology* 43(1), 30–47.

Murray, T. (ed.). 1999. *Time and Archaeology*. One World Archaeology 37. London: Unwin Hyman.

Myers, A. T. 2008. 'Between memory and materiality: an archaeological approach to studying the Nazi concentration camps'. *Journal of Conflict Archaeology* 4(1/2), 231–46.

Myers, A. 2011. 'The things of Auschwitz'. In A. Myers and G. Moshenska (eds), *Archaeologies of Internment*. New York: Springer, 75–88.

Myers, A. and Moshenska, G. (eds). 2011. *Archaeologies of Internment*. New York: Springer.

Myles, F. 2011. 'The Research and Production Plant, Parkgate, Dublin: archaeological investigation of a World War II munitions factory'. *Journal of Conflict Archaeology* 6(2), 73–96.

Mytum, H. 2011. 'A tale of two treatments: the materiality of internment on the Isle of Man in World Wars I and II'. In A. Myers and G. Moshenska (eds), *Archaeologies of Internment*. New York: Springer, 33–52.

Newman, P. 1981. *The Battle of Marston Moor*, Strettington, Anthony Bird Publications.

Odunbaku, J. B. and Alabi, R. A. 2010. 'Ditches and ramparts as evidenced of warfare defenses in 19th century Yorubaland: a view from Keesi, southwestern Nigeria'. *The African Diaspora Archaeology Newsletter*, March 2010. www.diaspora.uiuc.edu/news0310/news0310.htm. Accessed 17 April 2010.

Oosterbeek, L. 1997. 'War in the Chalcolithic? the meaning of the west Mediterranean hillforts'. In J. Carman (ed.), *Material Harm: Archaeological Studies of War and Conflict*. Glasgow: Cruithne Press, 116–32.

Osgood, R., Monks, S. and Toms, J. 2000. *Bronze Age Warfare*. Stroud: Sutton.

Otterbein, K. F. 1979. 'Huron vs. Iroquois: a case study in inter-tribal warfare'. *Ethnohistory* 26(2), 141–52.

Otto, T. 2006. 'Conceptions of warfare in western thought and research: an introduction'. In T. Otto, H. Thrane and H. Vandkilde (eds), *Warfare and Society: Archaeological and Social Anthropological Perspectives*. Aarhus: Aarhus University Press, 23–8.

Otto, T., Thrane, H. and Vandkilde, H. (eds). 2006a. *Warfare and Society: Archaeological and Social Anthropological Perspectives*. Aarhus: Aarhus University Press.

— (eds). 2006b. 'Warfare and Society: archaeological and social anthropological perspectives'. In T. Otto, H. Thrane and H. Vandkilde (eds), *Warfare and Society: Archaeological and Social Anthropological Perspectives*. Aarhus: Aarhus University Press, 9–19.

do Paço, A. 1962. 'Em tormo de Aljubarotta. I–O Problema dos ossos dos combatentes da batalha'. *Anais da Academia Portugesa da História* II12, 115–63.

—. 1963. 'The Battle of Aljubarotta'. *Antiquity* 37, 264–71.

Palubeckaité, Z., Jankauskas, R., Ardagna, Y., Macia, Y., Rigeade, C., Signoli, M. and Dutour, O. 2006. 'Dental status of Napoleon's Great Army's (1812) mass burial of soldiers in Vilnius: childhood peculiarities and adult dietary habits'. *International Journal of Osteoarchaeology* 16, 355–65.

Passmore, D. G. and Harrison, S. 2008. 'Landscapes of the Battle of the Bulge: WW2 field fortifications in the Ardennes Forests of Belgium'. *Journal of Conflict Archaeology* 4(1/2), 87–108.

Pearson, M. P. P. and Thorpe. I. J. N. 2005. *Warfare, Violence and Slavery in Prehistory: Proceedings of a Prehistoric Society Conference at Sheffield University*. BAR International Series 1374. Oxford: Archaeopress.

Persson, M. (ed.). 2011. *Skatås: utgrävningen av en minneslucka*. Lindome: Bricoleur Press.

Petty, G. and Petty, S. 1993. 'A geological reconstruction of the site of the Battle of Maldon'. In J. Cooper (ed.), *The Battle of Maldon. Fiction and Fact*, London and Rio Grande, The Hambledon Press, pp.159–69.

Piekarz, M. 2007. 'It's just a bloody field! Approaches, opportunities and dilemmas if interpreting English battlefields'. In C. Ryan (ed.), *Battlefield Tourism: History, Place and Interpretation*. Advances in Tourism Reserarch. Amsterdam: Elsevier, 29–47.

Pollard, T. 2001. '"*Place Ekowe in a state of defence*": the archaeological investigation of the British fort at KwaMondi, Eshowe, Zululand'. In T. Freeman and A. Pollard (eds), *Fields of Conflict: Progress and Prospects in Battlefield Archaeology, Proceedings of a Conference Held in the Department of Archaeology, University of Glasgow*, April 2000. BAR International Series 958. Oxford: Archaeopress, 253–64.

—. 2006. *Culloden Battlefield: Report on the Archaeological Investigation*. Glasgow, GUARD Report 1981, University of Glasgow.

—. 2007a. 'Burying the hatchet? The post-combat appropriation of battlefield spaces'. In L. Purbrick, J. Aulich and G. Dawson (eds), *Contested Spaces: Sites, Representations and Histories of Conflict*. Basingstoke: Palgrave Macmillan, 121–45.

—. 2007b. 'Seven eventful days in Paraguay: reconnoitering the archaeology of the War of the Triple Alliance'. In D. Scott, L. Babits and C. Haecker (eds), *Fields of Conflict: Battlefield Archaeology from the Roman Empire to the Korean War. Volume 2: Nineteenth and Twentieth Century Fields of Conflict*. Westport, CT: Praeger, 314–35.

—. 2008a. 'The archaeology of the siege of Leith, 1560'. *Journal of Conflict Archaeology* 4(1/2), 159–88.

—. 2008b. 'The archaeology of the siege of Fort William, 1746'. *Journal of Conflict Archaeology* 4(1/2), 189–230.

Pollard, T. and Banks, I. 2006a. 'Survey and excavation of an Anglo-Zulu War fort at Eshowe, KwaZulu-Natal, South Africa'. In T. Pollard and I. Banks (eds), *Past Tense: Studies in the Archaeology of Conflict*. Leiden: Brill = *Journal of Conflict Archaeology* 1, 133–80.

— (eds). 2006b. *Past Tense: Studies in the Archaeology of Conflict*. Leiden: Brill = *Journal of Conflict Archaeology* 1.

—. 2007. 'Not so quiet on the Western Front: progress and prospect in the archaeology of the First World War'. *Journal of Conflict Archaeology* 3(1), iii–xvi.

—. 2008. 'Archaeological investigation of military sites on Inchkeith Island'. *Journal of Conflict Archaeology* 4(1/2), 109–38.

Pollard, T., Barton, P. and Banks, I. 2007. *The Investigation of Possible Mass Graves at Pheasant Wood, Fromelles*. Glasgow: GUARD.

Portocarrero, G. 2011. 'Coastal defence systems in Arrábida, Portugal, during the early modern era: power and landscape'. *Post-Medieval Archaeology* 45(2), 291–306.

Pratt, G. M. 2007. 'How do you know it's a battlefield'? In Scott, D., Babits, L. and Haecker, C. (eds), *Fields of Conflict: Battlefield Archaeology from the Roman Empire to the Korean War* 2 vols. Westport, CT: Praeger, 5–38.

Prentice, G. and Prentice, M. C. 2000. 'Far from the battlefield: archaeology at Andersonville Prison'. In C. R. Geier and S. R. Potter (eds), *Archaeological Perspectives on the American Civil War*. Gainesville, FL: University Press of Florida, 166–87.

Price, J. 2004. 'The Ocean Villas Project: archaeology in the servoice of European remembrance'. In N. Saunders (ed.), *Matters of Conflict: Material Culture, Memory, and the First World War*. Abingdon: Routledge, 179–91.

—. 2006. 'Issues in managing the heritage of Great War in northern France and Belgium'. In T. Pollard and I. Banks (eds), *Past Tense: Studies in the Archaeology of Conflict*. Leiden: Brill = *Journal of Conflict Archaeology* 1, 181–96.

Pritchett, W. K. 1957. 'New light on Plataia'. *American Journal of Archaeology* 61, 9–28.

—. 1958. 'New light on Thermopylai'. *American Journal of Archaeology* 62, 203–13.

Purbrick, L. 2006. 'Long Kesh/Maze: Northern Ireland: public debate as historical interpretation'. In J. Schofield, A. Klausmeier and L. Purbroick (eds), *Remapping the Field: New Approaches in Conflict Archaeology*. Berlin: Westkreuz-Verlag, 72–80.

—. 2011. 'The last murals of Long Kesh: fragments of political imprisonment at the Maze Prison, Northern Ireland'. In A. Myers and G. Moshenska (eds), *Archaeologies of Internment*. New York: Springer, 263–84.

Raaflaub, K. and Rosenstein, N. 1999. *War and Society in the Ancient and Medieval Worlds*. Cambridge MA: Center for Hellenic Studies, Harvard University.

Randsborg, K. 1995. *Hjortspring. Warfare and Sacrifice in Early Europe*, Aarhus, Aarhus University Press.

Reznick, J. S. 2004. 'Prostheses and propaganda: materiality and the human body in the Great War'. In N. Saunders (ed.), *Matters of Conflict: Material Culture, Memory and the First World War*. London: Routledge, 51–61.

Reyna, S. 2009. 'Taking place: "new wars" versus global wars'. *Social Anthropogy/Anthropologie Sociale* 17(3), 291–317.

Rice, G. E. and Leblanc, S. A. (eds). 2001. *Deadly Landscapes: Case Studies in Prehistoric Southwestern Warfare*. Salt Lake City: University of Utah Press.

Roberts, N. A., Brown. J. W., Hammett, B. and Kingston, P. D. F. 2008. 'A detailed study of the effectiveness and capabilities of 18th century musketry on the battlefield'. *Journal of Conflict Archaeology* 4(1/2), 1–4.

Rost, A. 2007. 'Characteristics of ancient battlefields: the Battle of Varus AD9'. In D. Scott, L. Babits and C. Haecker (eds), *Fields of Conflict: Battlefield Archaeology from the Roman Empire to the Korean War* 2 vols. Westport, CT: Praeger, 50–7.

Rubio, X. 2008. *Almenar 1710: victòria anglesa a catalunya*. Camp de Mart 1. Barcelona: DIDPATRI.

Sage, A. and Evans, M. 2001. '"Grimsby Chums"' are found in war grave'. *The Times*, 20 June 2001.

Saitta, D. 2007. *The Archaeology of Collective Action*. The American Experience in Archaeological Perspective. Gainesville, FL: University of Florida Press.

Saitta, D., Walker, M. and Reckner, P. 2006. 'Battlefields of class conflict: then and now'. In T. Pollard and I. Banks (eds), *Past Tense: Studies in the Archaeology of Conflict*. Leiden: Brill = *Journal of Conflict Archaeology* 1, 197–214.

Saunders, N. 2001. 'Excavating memories: archaeology and the Great War 1914–2001'. *Antiquity* 76, 101–8.

—. 2003. *Trench Art: Materialities and Memories of War*. Oxford: Berg.

—. 2004. 'Material culture and conflict: the Great War 1914–2003'. In N. Saunders (ed.), *Matters of Conflict: Material Culture, Memory, and the First World War*. Abingdon: Routledge, 5–25.

—. 2007. 'The archaeology of Lawrence of Arabia (Jordan)'. In N. Saunders (ed.), *Killing Time: Archaeology and the First World War*, Stroud: Sutton, 225–29.

Saunders, R. 2002. 'Tell the truth: the archaeolopgy of human rights abuses in Guatemala and the former Yugoslavia'. In J. Schofield, W. G. Johnson and C. M. Beck (eds), *Matériel Culture: The Archaeology of Twentieth Century Conflict*. One World Archaeology 44. London: Routledge, 103–14.

Schofield, J. 2001. 'D-Day sites in England: an assessment'. *Antiquity* 75 287, 77–83.

—. 2004. *Modern Military Matters: Studying and Managing the Twentieth-Century Defence Heritage in Britain: A Discussion Document*. York: Council for British Archaeology.

—. 2005. *Combat Archaeology: Material Culture and Modern Conflict*. Duckworth Debates in Archaeology. Duckworth: London.

—. 2008. 'Heritage management, theory and practice'. In G. Fairclough, R. Harrison, J. Jameson and J. Schofield (eds), *The Heritage Reader*. London: Routledge, 15–30.

Schofield, J. and Anderton, M. 2000. 'The queer archaeology of Green Gate: interpreting contested space at Greenham Common Airbase'. *World*

Archaeology 322, 236–51.Schofield, J. and Cockroft, W. D. 2007. *A Fearsome Heritage: The Diverse Legacies of the Cold War*. London: UCL Press.

—. 2011. 'Hohenschönhausen: visual and material representations of a Cold War prison landscape'. In A. Myers and G. Moshenska (eds), *Archaeologies of Internment*. New York: Springer, 245–62.

Schofield, J., Carman, J. and Belford, P. 2012. *Archaeological Practice in Great Britain: The Heritage Handbook*. New York: Springer.

Schofield, J., Johnson, W. G. and Beck, C. M. 2002a. 'Introduction: material culture in the modern world'. In J. Schofield, W. G. Johnson and C. M. Beck (eds), *Matériel Culture: The Archaeology of Twentieth Century Conflict*. One World Archaeology 44. London: Routledge, 1–8.

— (eds). 2002b. *Matériel Culture: The Archaeology of Twentieth Century Conflict*. One World Archaeology 44. London: Routledge.

Scott, D. D., Fox, R. A., Connor, M. A. and Harmon, D. 1989. *Archaeological Perspectives on the Battle of the Little Big Horn*, Norman O and London: University of Oklahoma Press.

Scott, D., Babits, L. and Haecker, C. (eds). 2007. *Fields of Conflict: Battlefield Archaeology from the Roman Empire to the Korean War* 2 vols. Westport, CT: Praeger.

Seibert, E. K. M. and Parsons, M. T. 2000. 'Battling beyond First and Second Manassas: perseverance on a free African American farm site'. In C. R. Geier and S. R. Potter (eds), *Archaeological Perspectives on the American Civil War*. Gainesville, FL: University Press of Florida, 270–86.

Seitsonen, O. and Kunnas. L. 2009. 'Ahvola 1918: archaeological reconnaissance of a Finnish Civil War battlefield'. *Journal of Conflict Archaeology* 5(1), 57–80.

Shackel, P. 2000. '"Four years of hell": domestic life in Harper's Ferry during the Civil War'. In C. R. Geier and S. R. Potter (eds), *Archaeological Perspectives on the American Civil War*. Gainesville, FL: University Press of Florida, 217–28.

Shapiro, M. J. 1997. *Violent Cartographies: Mapping Cultures of War*. Minneapolis: University of Minnesota Press.

Shiels, D. 2007. 'Battle and siege maps of Elizabethan Ireland: blueprints for archaeologists'? *Journal of Conflict Archaeology* 3(1), 217–32.

Shepherd, D. J. 1999. 'The elusive warrior maiden tradition – bearing weapons in Anglo-Saxon society'. In J. Carman and A. Harding (eds), *Ancient Warfare: Archaeological Perspectives*. Stroud: Sutton, 219–48.

Signoli, M. et al. 2004. Discovery of a mass grave of Napoleonic period in Lithuania (1812, Vilnius). *Comptes Rendus Palaeovol* 3, 219–27.

Silverstein, J., Byrd, J. and Otineru. L. 2007. 'Hill 209: the last stand of Operation Manchu, Korea'. In D. Scott, L. Babits and C. Haecker (eds), *Fields of Conflict: Battlefield Archaeology from the Roman Empire to the Korean War* 2 vols. Westport, CT: Praeger, 417–28.

Sivilich, D. M. 2007. 'What the musket ball can tell: Monmouth Battlefield State Park, New Jersey'. In D. Scott, L. Babits and C. Haecker (eds), *Fields of Conflict: Battlefield Archaeology from the Roman Empire to the Korean War* 2 vols. Westport, CT: Praeger, 84–101.

Smith, S. D. 2000. 'The submarine *H. L. Hunley*: Confederate innovation and Southern icon'. In C. R. Geier and S. R. Potter (eds), *Archaeological Perspectives on the American Civil War*. Gainesville, FL: University Press of Florida, 29–42.

Stichelbaut, B. 2005. 'The application of Great War aerial photography in battlefield archaeology: the example of Flanders'. *Journal of Conflict Archaeology* 1, 235–43.

Stone, P. G. (ed.). 2011. *Cultural Heritage, Ethics and the Military*. Heritage Matters. Woodbridge: The Boydell Press.

Sturdy Colls, C. 2011. Holocaust Archaeology: archaeological approaches to landscapes of Nazi genocide and persecution. Unpublished PhD thesis, University of Birmingham, UK, September 2011.

Sutherland, T. 2007. 'Arrows point to mass graves: finding the dead from the battle of Towton 1461 AD'. In D. Scott, L. Babits and C. Haecker (eds), *Fields of Conflict: Battlefield Archaeology from the Roman Empire to the Korean War* 2 vols. Westport, CT: Praeger, 160–73.

—. 2009. 'Killing Time: challenging the common perceptions of three medieval conflicts – Ferrybridge, Dintingdale and Towton "the largest battle on British soil"'. *Journal of Conflict Archaeology* 5(1), 1–4.

Sutherland, T. and Holst, M. 2005. *Battlefield Archaeology: A Guide to the Archaeology of Conflict*. British Archaeology Jobs Resource.www.scribd. com/doc/404876/BATTLEFIELD-ARCHAEOLOGY-THE-ARCHAEO LOGY-OF-CONFLICT. Accessed 14 February 2012.

Talbot, G. and Bradley, A. 2006. 'Characterising Scampton'. In J. Schofield, A. Klausmeier and L. Purbroick (eds), *Remapping the Field: New Approaches in Conflict Archaeology*. Berlin: Westkreuz-Verlag, 43–8.

Tarlow, S. and West, S. (eds). 1999. *The Familiar Past? Archaeologies of Later Historical Britain*. London: Routledge.

Thomas, J. 2011. 'Archaeological investigations of Second World War prisoner of war camps at Fort Hood, Texas'. In A. Myers and G. Moshenska (eds), *Archaeologies of Internment*. New York: Springer, 147–70.

Thomas, R. J. C. 2003. 'PoW camps: what survives and where'. *Conservation Bulletin* 44, 18–21.

Thomas, R. and Stallibrass, S. 2008. *Feeding the Roman Army: The Archaeology of Production and Supply in NW Europe*. 17th Theoretical Roman Archaeology conference, London. Oxford: Oxbow.

Treherne, P. 1995. 'The warrior's beauty: the masculine body and self-identity in Bronze Age Europe'. *Journal of European Archaeology* 3.1, 105–44.

Trigg, J. 2007. 'Memory and memorial: a study of official and military commemoration of the dead, and family and community memory in Essex and East London'. *Journal of Conflict Archaeology* 3 1, 295–93.

Turney-High, H. 1949 [2nd (edn) 1971]. *Primitive War: Its Practice and Concepts*. Colombia: University of South Carolina Press.

Underhill, A. P. 2006. 'Warfare and the development of states in China'. In E. N. Arkush and M. W. Allen (eds), *The Archaeology of Warfare: Prehistories of Raiding and Conquest*. Gainesville, FL: University of Florida Press, 253–85.

van der Schriek, J. and van der Schriek, M. 2011. '"Up ewig Ungedeelt!" Schleswig-Holstein 1864–1920'. *Journal of Conflict Archaeology* 6(2), 146–72.

Vandkilde, H. 2006a. 'Archaeology and war: presentations of warriors and peasants in archaeological interpretations'. In T. Otto, H. Thrane and

H. Vandkilde (eds), *Warfare and Society: Archaeological and Social Anthropological Perspectives*. Aarhus: Aarhus University Press, 57–74.

—. 2006b. 'Warfare and gender according to Homer: an archaeology of an aristocratic warrior culture'. In T. Otto, H. Thrane and H. Vandkilde (eds), *Warfare and Society: Archaeological and Social Anthropological Perspectives*. Aarhus: Aarhus University Press, 515–28.

Vencl, S. 2006. 'Stone Age warfare'. In J. Carman and A. Harding (eds), *Ancient Warfare: Archaeological Perspectives*. Stroud: Sutton, 57–72.

Wainwright, A. 1998. 'Orford Ness'. In English Heritage (ed.), *English Heritage Monuments of War: The Evaluation, Recording and Management of Twentieth-Century Military Sites*. London: English Heritage, 11.

Weiss, L. 2011. 'Exceptional space: concentration camps and labor compounds in late nineteenth-century South Africa'. In A. Myers and G. Moshenska (eds), *Archaeologies of Internment*. New York: Springer, 21–32.

Wessex Archaeology 2008. *Shooters Hill, Greenwich, London: Archaeological Evaluation and Assesment of Results*. Report reference 65308.01. Salisbury: Wessex Archaeology.

Whitehorne, J. W. A., Geier, C. G. and Hofstra, W. R. 2000. 'The Sheridan Field Hospital, Winchester, Virginia, 1864'. In C. R. Geier and S. R. Potter (eds), *Archaeological Perspectives on the American Civil War*. Gainesville, FL: University Press of Florida, 148–65.

Whitford, T., and Pollard, T. 2009. 'For duty done: a WWI military medallion recovered from the mass grave site at Fromelles, Northern France'. *Journal of Conflict Archaeology* 5(1), 201–30.

Whorton, M. 2002. 'Evaluating and managing Cold War era historic properties: the cultural significance of US Air Force defensive radar systems'. In J. Schofield, W. G. Johnson and C. M. Beck (eds), *Matériel Culture: The Archaeology of Twentieth Century Conflict*. One World Archaeology 44. London: Routledge, 216–26.

Wilbers-Rost, S. 2007. 'Total Roman defeat at the Battle of Varus AD9'. In D. Scott, L. Babits and C. Haecker (eds), *Fields of Conflict: Battlefield*

Archaeology from the Roman Empire to the Korean War 2 vols. Westport, CT: Praeger, 121–32.

Wileman, J. 2009. *War and Rumours of War: The Evidential Base for the Recognition of Warfare in Prehistory*. BAR international series 1984. Oxford: Archaeopress.

Wills, H. 1985. *Pillboxes: A Study of UK Defences 1940*. London: Leo Cooper.

Wilson, L. K. nd *A Record of Fear*. Cambridge: The National Trust.

Wilson, R. J. 2007.'Archaeology on the Western Front: the archaeology of popular myths'. *Public Archaeology* 6(4), 227–41.

Zimmerman, L. 1997. 'The Crow Creek massacre, archaeology and prehistoric Plains warfare in comparative perspective'. In J. Carman (ed.), *Material Harm: Archaeological Studies of War and Conflict*. Glasgow: Cruithne Press, 75–94.

Index

Abánades, Spain 68
aerial photography 66, 70
Afghanistan 77-8
Ahsola, Finland 67
airfields 17
Alain-Fournier (French novelist) 64, 76
Aljubarotta, Portugal 44, 54
Almenar, Spain 57
amateurs 16-17
ambush 25
American Battlefields Protection Programme 7
American War of Independence 20
ammunition 68
Andersonville prison, USA 87
anthropology 2, 6, 9, 13-14, 18-19, 23-5, 35, 39-40, 46, 54, 59, 81, 88-90
Antietam, USA 84
archery 31
architecture 37, 69, 71, 72, 84
Ardennes 68
armour 31-3, 91
Arrábida coast, Portugal 84
Arras, France 64
arrowheads 25-6, 31, 49-50, 51
artworks 65
Auchonvilliers, France 66, 70

Balkans 78
barracks 69
barrage balloon 69
battle 39
battle axe 31
battlefield vi, 1, 7, 12, 40-61, 66-9
battlefield archaeology 10, 12, 15-16, 40-61

battlefield signature 50-2, 59, 61
Beaumont Hamel, France 66
Belgium 17, 20-1, 66
Berlin Wall 75
Bicester, England 70
Biology 34
Bletchley Park, England 70, 72
Blockhouse 83
Bloody Meadows Project vi, 90
boat burial 30-3
bombsite archaeology 69, 73, 79
Bosworth, England 49-50, 54
bows 31
Boyne, Ireland 57
Brooke, Richard 43
buildings 42, 43, 65, 68, 70, 80, 89
bullets 41, 47, 51, 84

case shot 47
castles 5
causes, of war 28-9, 34-5
cavalry 32
cemetery 25-6, 27, 36, 42, 65
   see also boat burial; human remains
chain mail 31
change 14, 24, 59, 70-1, 84, 92, 93
characterization 17, 69
Chemistry 43, 73, 93
children 38
chronology 9, 30, 65, 67, 78, 81-2, 99
churches, fortified 84, 93
citizenship 32
city-state 32
civilian experience 11, 12, 66, 69, 71, 73-5, 79-80, 84-5, 89, 92, 93-4, 96-7
class 11

Index

Cold War 1-2, 8, 17, 20, 71, 72-3, 75, 78, 79
collecting 43
collective action, archaeology of 11
Colorado Coalfield 'war' 67
combat archaeology 10-11, 12
community 2, 80, 92
concentration camps 74
confinement, archaeology of 73
context 39
co-operation with military 77-9
Council for British Archaeology (CBA) 17
craft 12
craters 17, 64
creation, war as 95
Crickley Hill, England 25-6
Critical Security Studies 3
Crow Creek massacre, USA 100
Cuba 71
Culloden, Scotland 57
cultural resource management 2, 10, 16-17, 63-5, 69, 76, 78, 79, 92-4
culture 15, 30, 34-5, 39

daggers 31
Dara, Syria 58
Darion, Belgium 25-6
decisiveness 15, 59
Defence of Britain Project 8, 17
defences 14, 17, 25-6, 27-8, 38-9, 69, 81, 82-3, 87, 91
demography 34
deposition 15, 59
destruction 14, 25-6, 27
deterrence 39
'Dirty' wars 8, 76, 78
discourse 3, 27, 33-8, 87-95
District Six, Capetown, South Africa 75
documentary sources 47, 52, 66, 68, 70
dugouts 17, 64, 66
Dukla Pass, Slovakia 68

Dundalk, Ireland 57
Dunnideer Fort, Scotland 28
Dybbøl, the, Denmark 58

Economics 35
Edgehill, England 48, 50-1, 57
Edwards Air Force Base, USA 70
elites 32, 37
Ename Center for Public Archaeology and Heritage Interpretation, Oudenaarde, Belgium 20
encampments 10, 12, 42
English Civil War 19, 43, 57
English heritage 44, 64, 92
environment 34-5, 39, 49, 86, 90
Eshowe, South Africa 58
establishments, military or naval 17, 42, 66, 69-73, 86, 89
see also barracks; encampments; logistics
ESTOC (European Studies of Terrains of Conflict) group vii, 93, 95
ethics 4, 65, 77-80, 99-100
European Union 17
Evansport, Virginia, USA 86
evidence 5, 8, 10, 11, 14, 25-33, 36-7, 39, 42, 44, 49, 59-60, 65-77
excavation 42-3, 48-9, 53, 66, 68, 70
experience 10-11, 66-7, 95-7
experiment 47, 71

Falklands Islands 77
female warrior 37
field names 43
Fields of Conflict conferences vii, 7, 9, 10, 19-20, 45, 54, 58, 78
fieldwalking 67, 68
Fitzgerald, Edward 43
Flanders vii, 20-1, 64, 96-8
Fontbregoua, France 25-6
Fort Beauséjour-Fort Cumberland, Canada 83
Fort George, Scotland 83
Fort Hood, Texas, USA 70, 74

fortification 82–3, 89
fortified churches 84, 93
Fort Nelson, Kentucky, USA 86
Fort Sam Houston, Texas, USA 70
Fromelles, France 66
frontiers 25–6
Fulford, England 49–50, 59
functionalism 15, 25–7, 30, 59, 90–1

Gallipoli, Turkey 66
Gebel Sahar, Egypt 25–6
gender 35–8
Geographical division
    see Nationalism
Geographical Information Systems
    (GIS) 70
Geography / geology 66
globalisation 2, 4, 18, 60–1
graves 25–6, 27, 31–2, 36, 42, 43–4,
    46, 48, 53–4, 69
    see also boat burial; cemetery;
    human remains
'Great Escape', the 74
Greece 31–2
Greenham Common, England 72, 89
grooming 37
Grossbeeren, Germany 58
guides 44
gun emplacements 69

Hambledon Hill, England 25–6
Harper's Ferry, Virginia, USA 85
Heritage / Heritage management
    see Cultural Resource Management
Hill 209
    Korea 76
historic battlefields 2, 7, 10, 15–16,
    18, 20–1, 40–61, 77, 78, 80
historic sources 48, 49, 52, 66
history 79
History of Conflict Archaeology 6–9,
    13–17, 23, 43–5, 63–5
Hjortspring, Denmark 30–3
Holocaust, the 8, 11

Holocaust archaeology 11, 73–4, 100
homesteads 84
Hoplite 31
horse 32
hospitals 12, 86
human remains 8, 14, 17, 25–8, 36–7,
    45, 48, 50, 53–4, 64–5, 76–7, 80, 88,
    99–100
human security 92
hypothesis testing 51–2

identity / identification 76, 93–8
Idstedt, Germany 58
Ieper, Belgium 66
incidence, of war 24–6, 35, 39
inherent military probability 51
innatist theory of war 14
internationalisation 2, 15–16, 18, 19,
    20–1, 60–1, 92–3, 95
internment, archaeology of 11, 73–4,
    79, 89
interpretation 25–6
inventory vii–iii, 7, 8
    see also register
Iraq 77–8
Ireland 19
Iron Age 5, 30–3
Isandhlwana, South Africa 58
Isle of Man 74

Jabal Abu al-Tyour, Jordan 68
Jacobite rebellion 19
Jarama, Spain 68
Jordan 68
Journal of Conflict Archaeology vii, 7,
    10, 19–20

Kalkriese, Germany 19, 49–50, 53–4,
    59
Kallaya Pit, Libya 67
Keesi, Yorubaland, Nigeria 84
Kit 70
Komárom, Hungary 58
Korea 78

Landguard Fort, England 83
landscape 17, 43–5, 50–1, 59, 65, 70, 80, 84–5, 90, 93, 97
Landskrona, Sweden 57
La Point du Jour, France 64
Lauenburg, Germany 57
LiDAR (Light Detection And Ranging) 83
Little Bighorn, Dakota, USA 7, 41, 45–6, 53–6, 68, 88
logistics 42, 69–73, 85–7
Long Kesh / Maze Prison, Northern Ireland 75
long-term 2–3, 14, 28–9, 100
looting 43, 53
Lützen, Germany 57

mace 31
Maldon, England 44–5
management 16
 see also Cultural Resource Management
Manassas, USA 85
Manzikert, Turkey 86
marriage 34
Marshall Islands 68
Marston Moor, England 44–5
martial arts 10
masculinity 36–7
massacre 25–6, 39
mass graves
 see cemeteries; Graves
material culture studies 12
memorialisation 12, 65, 68, 78, 93, 101
Messines, Belgium 66
metal detectors 41, 46–51, 57, 59, 67, 68, 93
metalworking 49–50, 59
methodology 14, 45–54, 59–60, 66–81
military archaeology 11
military history 2, 15–16, 35, 40, 44–6, 53, 56, 58–60, 90–2

military sociology 2, 15, 70, 89
Missile crisis, Cuban 71
modern conflict 2, 5, 7–11, 16–17, 63–80
monuments 5, 65, 78
morality 4
 see also Ethics
mortar 69
movement 15
multidisciplinarity 48

narrative 15
Naseby, England 43, 48, 57
nation state 91–2
National Army Museum, UK 10
nationalism 2, 6, 15–16, 18–21, 59–60, 95
National Park Service, USA 7, 92
native Americans 19–20
Northern Ireland 8, 75
Nuclear Testing Ground, Nevada, USA 64, 71–2, 89

occupation archaeology 11, 66, 73–5, 79
'Ocean Villas' Project *see* Auchonvilliers
Ofnet Cave, Germany 25–6
Oleye, Belgium 25–6
oral history 70
Orford Ness, England 71
origins 14, 38–9, 91, 100
orphan heritage 65
Oudenaarde, Belgium vii, 20–1, 51, 57, 96–8
outcomes, of war 28–30

pacified past 1, 6, 9, 23, 27
palisades 42
Palo Alto, Texas, USA 7, 45, 48, 50, 56
Paraguay 58
Parkgate, Dublin, Ireland 73
Passchendaele, Belgium 66
patterning 15, 46, 52, 59
peace camps 72, 89

Index 135

Peñol de Nochistlan, Mexico 57
period division 2, 3, 5, 6, 9, 13–17, 21, 81–2
perpetrators, archaeology of 94
pillboxes 8, 69
Pointe do Hoc, France 68
policy 21
Portugal 44, 93
post-Civil War battlefield pattern 46
post-deposition 43
practice of war 28–30
Predmost, Czech Republic 25–6
prehistory 1, 6, 7, 9, 10, 13–14, 18–19, 23–40, 64–5, 72–3, 77–8, 81, 87, 88, 90, 91, 94
preparations for war 28–30
preservation 17, 55, 60, 63, 69, 78, 94
prestige 34
Prisoner of War camps 12, 42, 73–4, 87, 89
processualism 46, 53
public interpretation 68, 93
public meaning 68, 76, 78, 94

Quantico Marine Corps base, USA 70
Québec, Canada 83
Quedlingburg, Germany 74

radar 71
RAF Bicester, England 70
RAF Scampton, England 70
raiding 25–6, 39
reburial 76
recording 94
    see also inventory
recovery, of dead 76
register of battlefields vii, viii, 7, 44, 92
religion 32, 72, 96
remembrance 74–5
repatriation 76
representation 12
rescue excavation 17
research questions 54

resistance 12, 66, 72–3, 74, 79, 89
    see also occupation archaeology; imprisonment
revolt 41
Rite de passage 31, 34
ritual 15, 23–4, 27, 28, 31, 33–4, 35, 39, 88
Robben Island, South Africa 75
Rouaix, France 25–6

sacrifice 30–3
St-Éxpury, Antoine 83
Saint Rémy la Colonne, France 64
Saipan 67
Salpa Line, Finland 68
Sandbjerget, Denmark 54
Sand Creek, USA 47
Scampton, RAF base, England 70
scatters 42–3, 45–50, 59
Scotland vii, 19
security 75
security studies 3, 20, 90–2
Sedgemoor, England 50, 57
selection 58–9
Serrre, River, France 66
settlement 35, 37, 84, 89, 91
shields 30–3, 36
Shooter's Hill, London, England 69
sieges 10, 15, 41, 61, 96, 100
signatures 50–2, 59, 61
skirmishes 41
social evolution 24, 32–3, 91
soldier 38, 46, 53–4, 96–8
Spanish Civil War 68–9, 74–6
spear / heads 30–3, 36, 49
Stalag Luft III 74
state, the 91–2
Stoke, England 43
strategic studies 3
structures 42
subterranean villages 84, 93
survey 42, 46–52, 57, 59, 64, 67, 68, 70, 84
survival 64

swords 28, 30–3, 36, 39, 49
Symbolism 25–6, 27, 72, 88

Talamanca, Spain 57
Talheim, Germany 25–6
taphonomy 43
technology 10–11, 12, 70, 71–2, 87, 91
terrain 50–1
testpits 43
Thirty Years' War 19
topography 43–5, 49–50, 52
Towton, England 45, 48, 50, 53–4, 88
trade 34
tradition 43
training areas 66
trauma 25–6, 28, 54, 88
Třebel, Czech Republic 57
trench art 12
trenches 17, 42, 64, 66–8, 70, 83
Trojan War 37
Troubles, Northern Ireland 8, 75
tunnels 67, 87

unification 2, 6
university/ies 1
uprisings 41
USA 19–20
US Civil War 20, 56–7, 84, 86, 89

vehicle 65

victimhood 37
Vietnam War 36, 78
Vilnius, Lithuania 54
Vimy Ridge, Belgium 66

Wadi Rum, Jordan 68
Wales vii
walls 42, 84
Waremme, Belgium 25–6
war / fare 1, 5, 23, 79, 90–6
Wars of the Roses 19, 43
warrior 10–11, 27–8, 31, 36–9, 46–7, 100
Washington Navy Yard, USA 70
weapons 10, 14, 15, 27, 30–3, 36–8, 42, 49, 50–1, 59, 66, 84
Winchester, Virginia, USA 86
Wisby, Denmark 54
women 37–8
World Archaeological Congress (WAC) 7, 77
worldview 95
World War I 2, 8, 11, 16–17, 20, 66, 68, 71, 73–4, 76, 78, 92–4
World War II 2, 8, 11, 16–17, 20, 64, 68–9, 73–4, 76, 78–9, 93

Yugoslavia 8

Zhoriv, Ukraine 57